KIDS' COMPUTER CAPERS

A Lothrop Computer Book

KIDS' COMPUTER CAPERS

INVESTIGATIONS FOR BEGINNERS

by Sandra Markle

illustrated by Stella Ormai

Updated Edition

Lothrop, Lee & Shepard Books • New York

I would like to say a special "thank you" to:
Bell Telephone Laboratories, Inc.
General Motors Corporation
Hewlett-Packard Company
Intel Corporation
IBM (International Business Machines Corporation)
3M (Minnesota Mining & Manufacturing Company)
Peachtree Software, Inc., an MSA Company
Taito Corporation of Tokyo, Japan
and the many others who offered help and encouragement to this project.

First Edition

4   5   6   7   8   9   10

Library of Congress Cataloging in Publication Data

Markle, Sandra.
    Kids' computer capers.

    Includes index.
    Summary: Presents the history of computers, investigates what computers can and cannot do, explores how they work, and explains how to operate a computer and write programs. Includes puzzles, activities, and mini-mysteries.
    1. Computers—Juvenile literature. 2. Programming (Electronic computers)—Juvenile literature. [1. Computers. 2. Programming (Electronic computers)] I. Ormai, Stella, ill. II. Title.
QA76.23.M37 1983   001.64   83-807
ISBN 0-688-02378-9 (lib. bdg.)   ISBN 0-688-02429-7 (pbk.)

For Bill,
Scott,
and Holly,
who share the dream

CONTENTS

Escape

"Gotcha!" McThug's strong arms wrap around you. You're snapped back against the big man's chest. You try to yank free, but you can't.

"Thought you could get to the treasure ahead of us, huh?" Peterson pokes a skinny finger in your face.

"I'm going to find the gold," you say, wiggling hard. "I've got the map showing where it's buried."

"Not anymore." Peterson plucks the map from your hand. "Now *we've* got the map."

Suddenly McThug swings you over his shoulder. You try to kick, but the big man's hands are holding your legs. You hit his back with your fists. The blows don't bother McThug.

"Put me down," you shout. "Let me go!"

Peterson scurries ahead, carrying a flashlight, as McThug starts down a steep flight of stairs.

The old house is on the Georgia coast, not too far from Savannah. It was built by the famous pirate Red Beard. He supposedly buried a treasure in this house. And you found a map showing where that treasure is buried.

You don't know how McThug and Peterson found out about the map. You *do* know that these are dangerous men, and that you are in trouble.

You hear a creaking sound as a metal door is opened. Then you are dumped onto a cold stone floor.

"That'll keep you out of the way." McThug pushes the door shut.

You scramble to your feet and rush to the small window in the door. You have to stretch on your tiptoes to look through the opening.

"Let me out," you plead.

"Sorry." Peterson doesn't sound sorry. "Here." The skinny man pokes a flashlight in your face.

You grab it and pull it through the opening. "Will you come back and let me out?"

"Maybe," answers Peterson.

"Don't count on it," snorts McThug.

Then they leave. You're alone in the dark. You're trembling so hard that you have trouble turning on the flashlight. Following the narrow beam of light, you look around.

You are in a storage room. The walls are made of stone blocks. There are no windows. The door is locked and won't budge when you push on it. The only thing in the room is a big wooden box.

Maybe the box has something in it that will help you get out. You lift the lid. The box is empty.

Then you see a crack in the stone wall behind the box. You shove the box aside. There is a hole. It's small, but big enough to squeeze through. Dropping to your knees, you crawl through the hole.

You are in a cavelike room. You stand up. Ahead of you there are six tunnels leading into darkness.

This is your chance to escape. One of the tunnels must lead out. But which one? Taking a deep breath, you try to decide which tunnel to take.

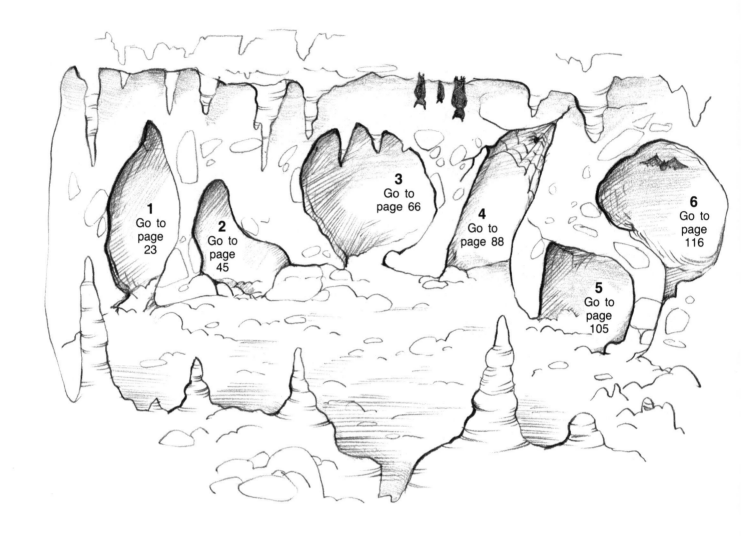

1
Go to
page
23

2
Go to
page
45

3
Go to
page 66

4
Go to
page 88

5
Go to
page
105

6
Go to
page
116

Escape isn't a real computer game, but it could be. The action is the same. You are involved. The choices are yours.

One tunnel will let you escape. The others are dead ends and will force you to double back. In every case, danger awaits you.

While you're working on finding the way out, read the rest of *Kids' Computer Capers*. You'll discover a little of the history of computers, investigate what computers can and cannot do, and explore how a computer works. You'll plunge into the basics of operating a computer. And you'll find out how to write programs that will make the computer follow your orders. A computer even generated the design shown in stop-action on the chapter-title pages. Flip through them and watch the design build. Throughout the book you'll find jokes, games, things to make, and lots more mysteries—escape, if you can, but don't miss the rest of the fun on your way out.

A Little History

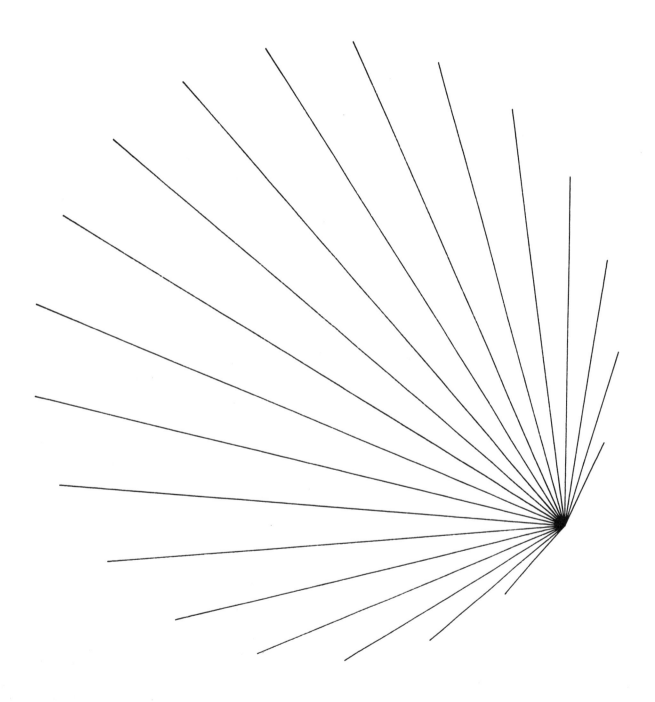

(Courtesy of Peachtree Software, Inc., an MSA Company)

Sticks and Stones and Pictures That Counted

In the early years B.C. (before computers), keeping track of what you owned wasn't a problem. Even kings and tax collectors could get by with counting bags of stones or making scratches on a clay tablet. Tying knots on a leather thong—one knot per sheep, or whatever—was also a popular method of counting.

Tally sticks were used like receipts. If you bought twelve chickens, your tally stick had twelve notches.

1 =	|	Staff
10 =	∧	Heel (or arch)
100 =	⌒	Coiled rope
1,000 =		Lotus flower
10,000 =		Finger
100,000 =		Tadpole
1,000,000 =		Surprised man

The ancient Egyptians used hieroglyphics, a picture language. On the left is a sample of the pictures they used for showing numbers.

Mini-Mystery

What number is this?

(See page 16.)

How About a Game of Exchequer?

The Exchequer was actually the king's counting house in old England. The building got its name because, as the king's money was counted, piles of counters were moved around on a checkered cloth.

IX + XI = ?

Roman numerals were hard to work with. So the ancient Romans used the abacus to add, subtract, multiply, and divide. The first column on the right of the abacus showed ones. The farthest column on the left showed trillions. Beads above the crossbar were worth five times the ones below. Beads at the bar were in use.

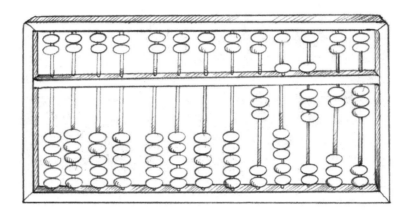

The ancient Chinese system of numbering was even harder to work with than Roman numerals. The abacus became popular in the Far East too. And it remained the main tool for solving number problems until computers became small, fast, and inexpensive enough to be owned by small businesses.

ROMAN NUMERALS		CHINESE NUMBERS	
1 = I	6 = VI	1 = 一	6 = 六
2 = II	7 = VII	2 = 二	7 = 七
3 = III	8 = VIII	3 = 三	8 = 八
4 = IV	9 = IX	4 = 四	9 = 九
5 = V	10 = X	5 = 五	10 = 十

The Hindus developed the number system used most often today. This is called the decimal system: 1, 2, 3, 4, 5, 6, 7, 8, 9, and 0. One reason this system became popular is that it has zero—a symbol for nothing.

You Can Count on Me, Dad

Blaise Pascal's father was the tax-court judge in Clermont-Ferrand, France. It was a hard job that meant spending long hours adding and subtracting columns of numbers.

Blaise wanted to make life easier for his father. So in 1641, he invented a machine that could add and subtract. The numbers to be added were dialed in. The answer showed up in the windows at the top. When numbers were to be subtracted, the dials were turned backward.

The Pascaline, as the machine was called, made solving number problems a little easier, but it never became very popular. Adding and subtracting with this machine wasn't, in fact, any faster than calculating in your head.

Math Lover

Blaise Pascal's father didn't want him to study math until he had mastered Greek and Latin. So Blaise secretly taught himself geometry when he was twelve.

Blaise Pascal (1623–1662) was only eighteen when he invented the Pascaline.

Mini-Mystery Answer
203,142

An Idea to Hang On to

Gottfried Leibniz (1646–1716) built an improved model of the Pascaline. His machine worked faster and could multiply and divide as well as add and subtract.

Leibniz also developed a new way of counting called the <u>binary</u> <u>system</u>. *Bi* means "two," and in the binary system, all numbers are symbolized by groups of just two numbers—zero and one.

$$1 = 0001 \qquad 2 = 0010 \qquad 3 = 0011 \qquad 4 = 0100 \qquad 5 = 0101$$

Because it was a lot easier to work with decimal numbers, Leibniz's binary system was forgotten for almost two hundred years. It wasn't until the 1940's that inventors discovered that what had been too hard for people was perfect for machines.

The binary system (for numbers and, later, for an alphabet) became the key to making a language that a computer could store and understand.

(Turn to page 63 to translate the robot's message.)

Gearing Up

The early calculating machines, including the Pascaline and Leibniz's improved version, all worked with cogwheels and gears. You can see how they operated by making a model.

First collect these materials:

> two large empty Styrofoam spools (from sewing thread)
> a clean Styrofoam meat tray (about 8 inches by 4 inches)
> fifteen straight pins
> two nails (2½ inches long) with large heads
> a piece of plywood (about 10 inches by 6 inches)
> a hammer
> scissors

1 With the scissors, cut a circle (about 4 inches in diameter) and three squares (each big enough to cover the end of the spool) from the tray.

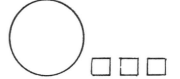

2 Stack the plywood, one spool, two squares, and the circle, as shown. Then poke a nail through the top square and spool. Using the hammer, send the nail through the Styrofoam wheel, bottom square, and plywood. You may need an older person's help with this. When you're finished, be sure the wheel can turn freely.

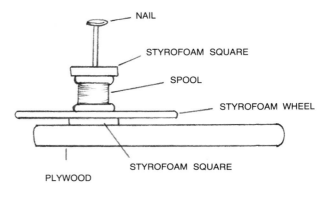

3 Poke about ten pins into the edge of the Styrofoam wheel. Space them evenly all the way around. Poke the remaining pins into the second spool near the bottom, as shown.

4 Put a Styrofoam square over the top of the second spool. Place this spool close enough to the big

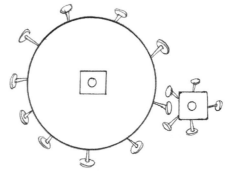

wheel that the pins meet. Nail it in position, as before. When you spin the spool, what happens?

In real life, the Pascaline and other early calculating machines were based upon the decimal system and the gears were designed with a ten-to-one ratio. One thing that made these early machines hard to build was how exact their size and shape had to be for them to work properly.

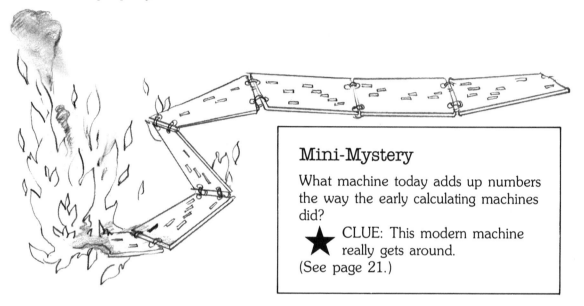

Mini-Mystery

What machine today adds up numbers the way the early calculating machines did?

★ CLUE: This modern machine really gets around.

(See page 21.)

Hot Moment in History

One night in 1801, angry silkweavers in Lyons, France, set fire to Joseph Jacquard's home. Jacquard and his family were able to escape unharmed, but they lost everything. Among the things that were destroyed was Jacquard's latest invention—an automatic loom.

It was the loom that the weavers had wanted to destroy. Joseph Jacquard (1752–1834) had found a way to use punched cards hooked together in a long chain to control the pattern that the loom produced. The silk weavers were afraid that the loom would take away their jobs.

Jacquard rebuilt his card-controlled loom and gradually convinced people to try it. By 1812, there were over 11,000 Jacquard looms in France. Lyons became famous worldwide for its finely woven silks. Joseph Jacquard's idea of using punched cards also helped the men who were trying to invent better calculating machines.

Father of the Computer

Charles Babbage (1792–1871) believed that he could build a machine that would handle a series of number problems and print the answers. The British government believed he could do it too and gave him the money he needed to build his machine.

The Difference Engine was a good idea. But after ten years of trying, it still didn't work. The problem was making the hundreds of metal rods, cogwheels, and gears needed to put the machine together. The British government took one look at the tons of scrap metal and refused to give Babbage any more money.

But Babbage wouldn't give up. Changing his plans somewhat, he tried to build a steam-powered machine with a calculating unit and a memory unit. He wanted to use punched cards to feed orders and information into the machine.

If Babbage's idea had worked, his machine would have been the first modern <u>computer</u>. But it didn't work because the parts just couldn't be made exactly enough to do the job.

Charles Babbage's machines failed, but his ideas succeeded. Today he is called the father of the computer because he inspired later inventors to build what he could only imagine.

And the Winner Is . . .

When the 1880 U.S. census was recorded, it had taken government clerks seven years to total the numbers. Unless someone could figure out an easier way to count noses, the 1890 census was going to be an impossible job.

A contest was held to see if someone could come up with a better and faster way to record and count the census information.

Herman Hollerith's (1860–1929) tabulating machine was the winner. With it, the information could be checked by a card scanner and recorded by counting dials. Six weeks after census day, the total population of the United States in 1890 was announced—62,622,250.

Do you know what the population of the United States is today? Check a recent atlas. That total will have been recorded by a computer.

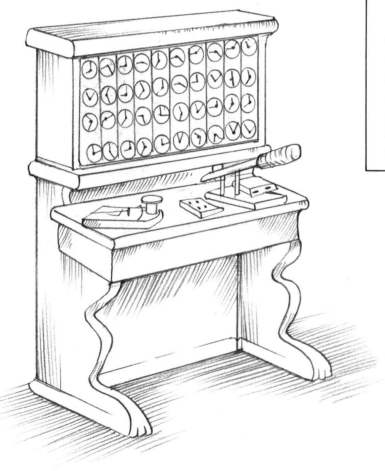

Mini-Mystery Answer

The odometer in a car works the same way as the early calculating machines. Look on a car's dashboard. The odometer shows how many miles the car has been driven.

When the card scanner was pulled down, pins went through any open holes into cups of mercury. This completed electric circuits leading to the counting dials.

Mystery Person

Do you have someone in your family who secretly loves chocolate, thinks the best place to go for a vacation is the beach, and likes to watch mysteries on TV? You can use Hollerith's card system to find that mystery person.

You'll need one 5 × 7 index card for each person in your family. Use a hole punch and a pen to make each card like the one in the picture. Don't forget yourself!

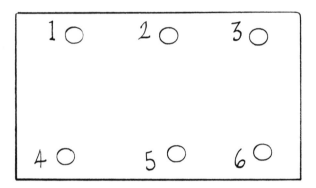

The numbers match these questions:

1. Do you eat chocolate at least once a week?
2. Is the beach your favorite vacation spot?
3. Do you like to go to baseball games?
4. Do you like to watch cartoons on TV?
5. Do you like to watch mystery shows on TV?
6. Would you rather eat out than eat at home?

Let each person mark the answers on his or her own card by cutting open the outside edge of the hole each time their answer is *no*. When the answer is *yes*, the hole should not be cut.

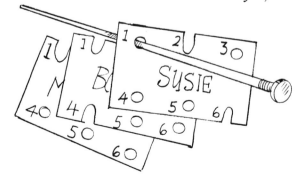

Stack the cards with the names face up. Use a straw, a pipe cleaner, or a knitting needle to poke through the *yes* hole for question 1. Shake. The cards left hanging on the probe belong to the people in your family who love chocolate.

Next, using only the chocolate fans' cards, stick the probe through the hole for question 2. Shake. Any cards remaining belong to chocolate lovers who like to vacation at the beach.

Finally, stack these cards and stick the probe through the hole of question 5. Shake. Whose card is left?

Aha! The chocolate-loving, beach-vacationing mystery watcher in your family is . . .

Now track down the person who isn't crazy about chocolate, likes to go to baseball games, and loves to eat out.

Tunnel One

You are walking down the tunnel. The air is cool and damp, but you are sweating. You have the feeling that someone or some*thing* is watching you.

Suddenly the flashlight's beam splashes against a rock wall. Dead end.

Then you hear a hiss. You look up.

A huge white snake is coiled on a rock ledge above your head. The snake's eyes gleam silver in the dim light. Its tongue flicks in and out.

Slowly you step back—one step and then another. The snake lifts its head to strike.

You swing around and run. Heart pounding, legs pumping, you run back to the cavelike room. Still shaking, you choose another tunnel.

(Go back to page 12 and try again.)

Marking the Beginning

Herman Hollerith founded the Tabulating Machine Company to market his inventions. This company grew and joined other companies until it became the International Business Machines Corporation—IBM. Heard of it?

In the early 1940's IBM helped launch the computer age by funding the building of the Mark I at Harvard University.

Switched on for the first time in 1943, the Harvard Mark I's job was to solve problems for the navy.

(Courtesy of International Business Machines Corporation)

Designed by Howard Aiken (1900–1973), the Mark I was built with stainless steel and glass so it would look like a super machine. But the "electronic brain" was a computer dinosaur. Fifty-five feet long and eight feet high, it had about one million parts. Despite its size, it could only do three additions per second. Today's average microcomputer can handle 270,000 instructions per second.

24

ENIAC (Faster than Thought—When It Worked)

The U.S. entered World War II in 1941 with new long-range guns that had not yet been tested. As a result, ballistics tables were needed to tell the gunners at what angle to set the big guns to hit targets at various distances.

A group of women took on the job of making these tables, but what a job! Solving all the mathematical problems necessary to find just one number for one table took twelve hours. The ballistics tables needed the answers for 3,000 similar problems.

John Mauchly (1907–1980) and J. Presper Eckert, Jr. (1919—), convinced the government that a computer was needed to make these calculations. With government funding, the team went to work to develop this time-saving machine.

The completed computer, ENIAC (Electronic Numerical Integrator and Computer), was much faster than the Mark I, but building it took thirty months. By the time it was ready, the war was over.

ENIAC first showed off its speed for the public in 1946 by multiplying 97,367 by itself five thousand times. The computer had the correct answer in less than half a second. Unfortunately, speed wasn't everything. ENIAC needed 18,000 vacuum tubes to operate. If any tube burned out, the entire computer shut down.

ENIAC's 18,000 tubes acted just like light bulbs and used a lot of electricity. When the computer was turned on, lights in parts of nearby Philadelphia dimmed.

As the machine worked, its tubes gave off a lot of heat. To keep ENIAC cool, an air-conditioning system big enough to cool the Empire State Building had to be installed.

ENIAC could be given orders, but it could only solve problems for ballistics tables and for tables of weather information. To do any other kind of job, ENIAC had to have some of its parts rewired.

Stored Memory

The early electronic computers could not work very fast for two reasons:

1. The computer had to wait for a person to feed it information and orders.
2. The computer could not switch from one set of orders to another.

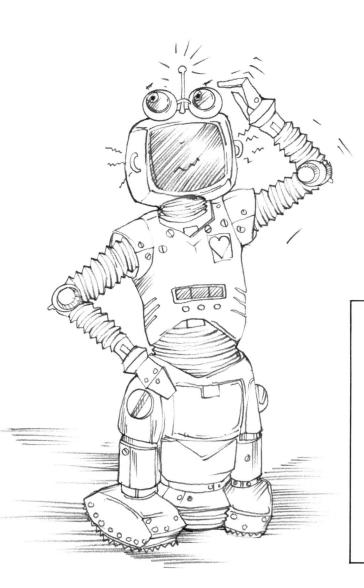

U.S. mathematician John von Neumann's (1903–1957) idea solved both problems. He said that computers needed "stored memory." With stored memory, information and orders can be fed to a machine and kept there until needed. The computer can use stored memory as fast as its electrical parts can work. The only thing to slow it down is the amount of storage space it has available for information and instructions.

Mini-Mystery

Every day, just as a plane leaves Miami, Florida, bound for London, England, a plane leaves London bound for Miami. A plane leaves London every hour on the hour, heading for Miami. The flight takes six hours.

How many planes from London will the Miami flight pass by the time it lands in London? (Check yourself on page 49.)

The Secret of Colossus

While ENIAC was still having its circuits hooked together, another computer was secretly at work helping the war effort.

Clackety-clackety-clackety-click. The man standing near Colossus smiled and then nodded.

"Colossus has done it again," he announced proudly. "Let's get this message off to Churchill in London. We now know Hitler's new attack plan."

Moments later a courier rushed from the country house in Hertfordshire, England, called Bletchley Park. The courier carried a large envelope stamped TOP SECRET. Any message from Colossus was very important. Colossus was a computer designed by Alan Turing (1912–1954) and a team of mathematicians.

With the help of the Polish underground, the British had stolen one of the Germans' encoding machines. Encoding means changing a readable message into an unreadable code. Only someone who knew how to decode (translate) the message could read it. So each time the German high command changed their code, Colossus went to work. Scanning at an amazing rate, Colossus was able to break the new codes much faster than people could.

When Churchill opened the envelope, he found the translated message written in another kind of code.

"Bring me a broom," thundered the Prime Minister.

Why did the Prime Minister need a broom? What was the coded message?

(This message from Colossus wasn't real, but the computer was. It helped England defend itself from attacks. For the answer to the mystery, see page 30.)

Bits and Bytes

Computers store numbers and information in binary code by having electronic switchlike spots *on* or *off*. These spots are called bits. The word bit comes from *binary* dig*it*.

The binary system originally developed by Gottfried Leibniz was perfect for the computer. With this system, as you remember, numbers were shown as groups of zeros and ones. A zero could be stored by a tube (and later, a transistor, or electronic switch) being *off*. A one could be stored by a tube or transistor being *on*.

Using this method, a code called ASCII (see page 63) was invented to store letters and symbols. With ASCII and other computer codes, groups of eight bits are usually used to store each number, letter, or symbol. A byte is a group of eight bits.

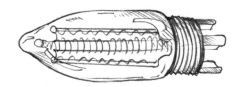

Memory Boost

Although ENIAC had 18,000 tubes, only a few hundred were used as memory. The rest handled general operations. And in order to "remember," ENIAC's tubes had to remain on—burning themselves out—as spots of stored information. To be really useful, computers needed bigger memories, but that seemed impossible. Machines like ENIAC already filled gymnasium-size rooms, and each one used a city's worth of power. Computers also needed more reliable memories. Whenever any one of ENIAC's tubes burned out, the giant's entire memory went blank.

As early as 1947, William Shockley (1910—), John Bardeen (1908—), and Walter Brattain (1902—) were working on these problems at Bell Telephone Laboratories. What they invented in 1948 and perfected during the early 1950's was called the transistor. Probably more than any other single invention, the transistor changed what computers were like and how well they could remember.

The transistor was made of silicon (a material that is the main ingredient in sand), which is a semiconductor. Unlike a vacuum tube, the transistor needed only a small amount of electricity to turn *on*. Transistors used much less electricity, gave off very little heat, and were tiny. It took a stack of two hundred transistors to equal the size of the smallest vacuum tube.

With the invention of the transistor, computers could be made much smaller and still have big memories. Although ENIAC could store only a hundred or so bits, computers with transistors could have memories of millions—and eventually, billions—of bits. Transistors also made it possible for computers to have long-lasting, reliable memories.

No longer merely giant calculators, computers suddenly had the space and the ability to store, sort, and test the vast amounts of facts and data that were being generated by the government and big businesses.

(Courtesy of Bell Telephone Laboratories, Inc.)

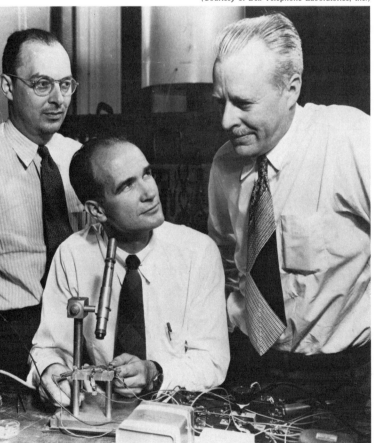

William Shockley, John Bardeen, and Walter Brattain received the 1956 Nobel Prize in Physics for their invention of the transistor.

Output

CONDUCTORS: such as gold, copper, and aluminum, allow electricity to flow through them freely.

INSULATORS: such as glass and rubber, do not allow electricity to flow through.

SEMICONDUCTORS: such as silicon, let a small amount of electricity squeeze through.

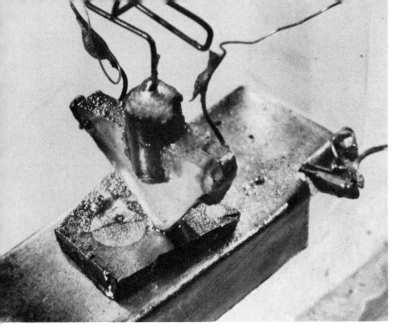

This early transistor, like modern ones, made electrical signals stronger by passing them through the solid silicon disk.

(Courtesy of Bell Telephone Laboratories, Inc.)

Made with Care

While a finished transistor could take a lot more rough handling and last a lot longer than a vacuum tube, its production required more care. Lint, oil droplets, sweat, and stray hairs could ruin a transistor.

Transistor factories had to be as clean as hospitals. And the people making the transistors had to wear caps and gowns like doctors and nurses.

At first the wires were attached to the silicon wafers by people looking through microscopes. This was very hard work.

Then, in 1959, IBM developed a machine that could produce 1,800 transistors per hour. Once transistors were cheap as well as small and dependable, they became part of televisions, radios, hearing aids, and many other products in addition to computers.

"Secret of Colossus" Answer

When Churchill got the broom, he held the end of the message tape with the arrow against the handle. Then he wrapped the tape around the handle. The letters fit into place.

WILL
BOMB
LONDON
AT
MIDNIGHT

You can use this code to send your own messages. Use adding-machine tape or cut strips of paper and tape them together to form a long strip. Wrap the paper around a broom handle or a paper-towel tube. Then print your message straight down the length of the strip. When uncoiled, the words will be unreadable.

Be sure to let your friend know how to read your message and what to wrap it around. To be read, the paper must be wrapped around something that has the same diameter as the rod shape you used for writing the message.

The Shrinking Computer

While the computer's memory was growing, its bulky frame was shrinking. And since electrical signals now had less distance to travel through the computer's circuits (pathways for electricity to follow), information and numbers could be processed much faster.

The transistor had done a lot to change the computer, but in the 1960's the United States and Russia were in a race to launch men into space. Missile and satellite programs needed more complex electronic systems that wouldn't take up any more room, weigh more, or use more power than simpler systems. Eventually an integrated circuit was developed with all the circuit's parts being formed by a complex process of diffusing chemicals into silicon or by depositing thin films of materials onto silicon. Each circuit junction became a switch—like a transistor—to control the flow of electricity. The <u>chip</u>, as it was nicknamed, made it possible for miniature computers to be built with as much—and eventually more—memory as earlier, much larger machines.

How a Chip Is Made

In the design phase, engineers plan the size and location of every circuit element on the chip. Then photomasks, patterns that will be used to create the circuit pathways and elements, are produced. Detailed, computer-drawn plots of the photomasks are greatly enlarged so they can be checked for mistakes. Any flaw could affect the chip's ability to store and handle information. When the photomasks are ready, they are photographically reduced to the tiny size of a finished chip and then reproduced side-by-side many times in a process called "step and repeat."

To make chip production easier, silicon loaves are first sliced into thin wafers rather than diced immediately into tiny chips. Many chips are formed on each wafer and cut apart later.

A film of photoresist is spread evenly over the wafers' surface, and, using special lenses, a scaled-down photomask is then projected over each wafer. After being exposed to ultraviolet light, the wafers are dipped in an acid bath. The parts of the photoresist that were shielded from the light are washed away. Unshielded areas remain and harden to form outlines of circuits. Then the wafers are baked in an oxygen furnace. Oxygen reacts with the silicon to form an insulating layer of glass on the circuits.

Here a worker checks a photomask for flaws.

(Courtesy of Intel Corporation)

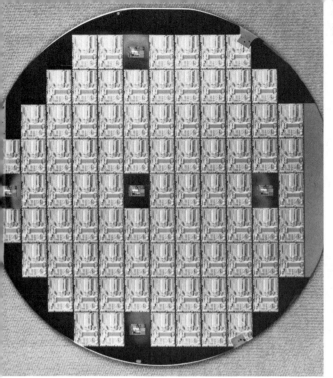

sy of Intel Corporation)

Many chips are formed on each silicon wafer and sliced apart later.

(Courtesy of Intel Corporation)

The wafers are spun rapidly to spread a film of photoresist evenly over the surface.

A worker puts silicon wafers into a "boat" in preparation for their acid bath. Since dust can ruin a chip, work is done in a "clean room." Workers dress like members of a surgical team.

(Courtesy of Intel Corporation)

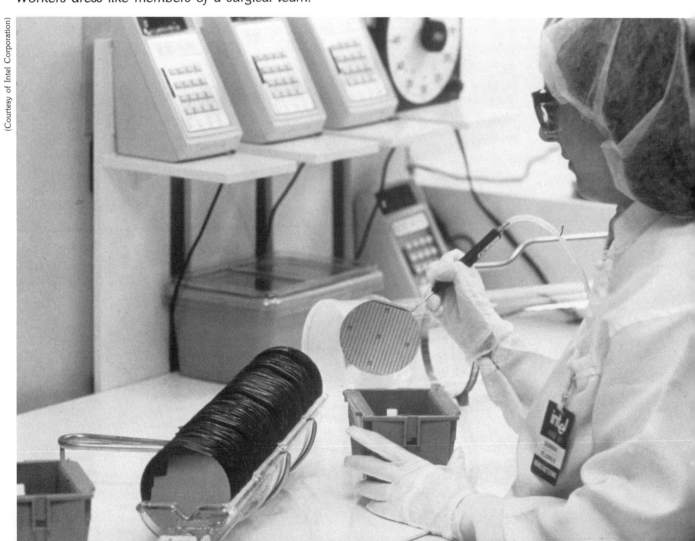

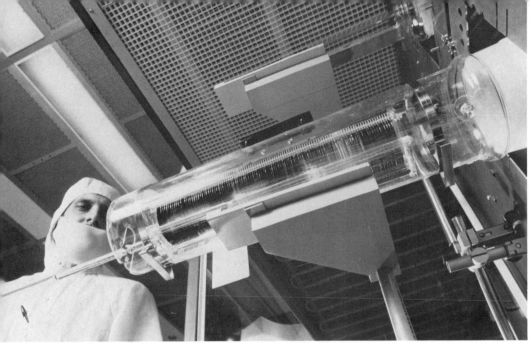

Inside the oxygen furnace, the wafers are heated to over 1000° Celsius in a diffusion furnace.

(Courtesy of International Business Machines Corporation)

This process can be repeated to form additional circuit patterns. Circuit elements, such as transistors, are formed on the wafer by depositing special chemicals, implanting charged particles called ions, or diffusing key impurities.

Finally the wafers are inspected through a microscope for flaws and scratches. The circuits are also tested electrically. The finished chips have as many as 65,000 circuit junctions. Each junction is one spot for storing information.

This worker is looking for flaws and scratches that could keep the chips from working properly.

The final test is to check the electrical circuits.

(Courtesy of Intel Corporation) (Courtesy of Bell Telephone Laboratories, Inc.)

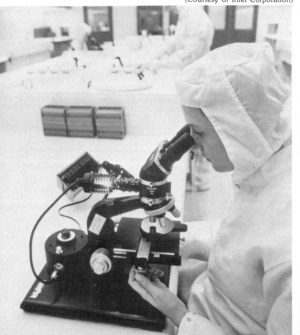

Tiny enough to fit through the eye of a needle, this chip has as much computing power as the giant computers built only a few years ago.

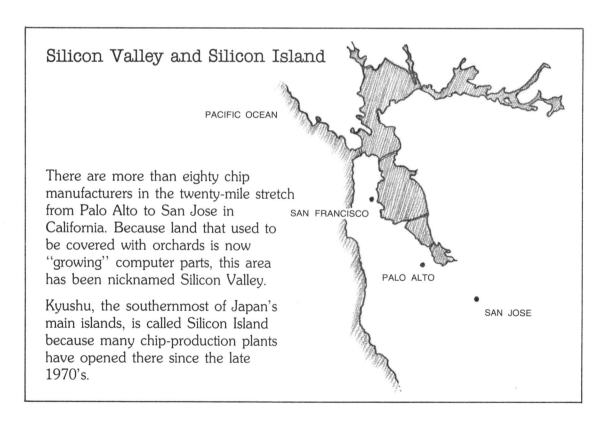

Silicon Valley and Silicon Island

PACIFIC OCEAN

SAN FRANCISCO

PALO ALTO

SAN JOSE

There are more than eighty chip manufacturers in the twenty-mile stretch from Palo Alto to San Jose in California. Because land that used to be covered with orchards is now "growing" computer parts, this area has been nicknamed Silicon Valley.

Kyushu, the southernmost of Japan's main islands, is called Silicon Island because many chip-production plants have opened there since the late 1970's.

Lost in a Chip

Make your own chip maze, using these two circuit masks. First trace mask A. Then, lining up the arrows, trace mask B over mask A.

Now the circuits are complete. Find the path the electric current will follow through the circuits, beginning at either arrow. Watch out for closed junctions.

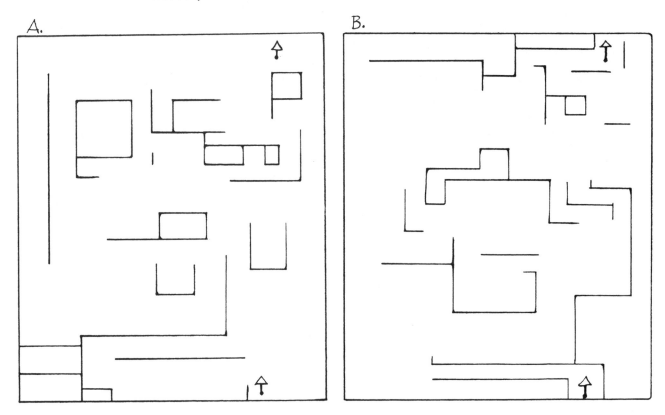

A.

B.

Computer on a Chip

It became possible to cram more and more transistors and circuits onto a chip. And the chip became a microprocessor—a computer on one silicon wafer. Inexpensive, and needing no more power than a flat, thumbnail-size battery could supply, the microprocessor was ready to slip inside many familiar machines and become the control center of some brand-new ones.

The computer had changed from a giant that primarily aided big businesses and governments to a tiny, but powerful, tool for everyone's use.

Computers at Work

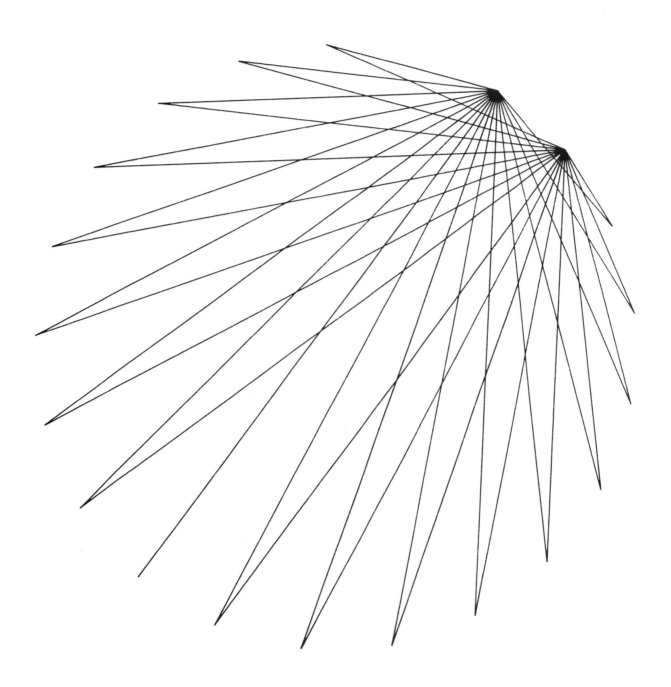

Secret Computers

There are twelve computers hidden inside machines in this picture. Make a list of where you think the computers are hiding. Check yourself on page 40.

Each of these secret computers is a special-purpose computer with only one job. The <u>program</u> for that job is burned into the computer's memory circuits and can't be changed very easily.

Automatic teller machines found at many banks are also special-purpose computers. Their only job is to collect or give out money.

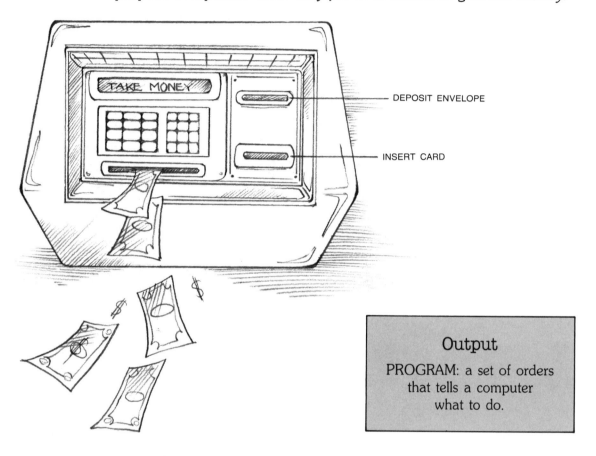

DEPOSIT ENVELOPE

INSERT CARD

> ## Output
> PROGRAM: a set of orders that tells a computer what to do.

To use the banking machine, the person puts a card that has a coded strip of magnetic tape on it into the card reader. Then the customer types in a code number representing his or her account. The teller machine's card reader feeds the code on the card's magnetic tape into the computer. If the two codes match, the computer searches its records for the person's account information.

To withdraw money, the person presses the withdrawal key and types in an amount. If there is enough money on account, the computer orders a payoff, and the money cartridge begins to move along the transport belt. The money passes a photosensor, which checks to make sure only individual bills are being given out. If two bills are stuck together, the money is dumped into a reject bin, and the machine starts the payoff process all over again. Usually only $20 and $5 bills can be handled by the automatic banking machines. Each machine can store as much as $50,000.

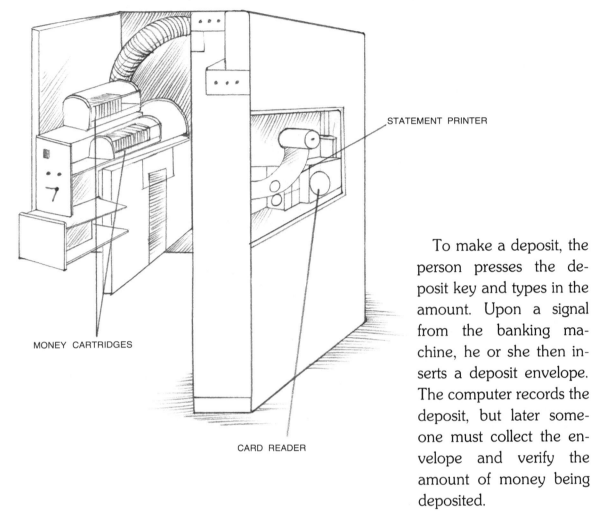

STATEMENT PRINTER

MONEY CARTRIDGES

CARD READER

To make a deposit, the person presses the deposit key and types in the amount. Upon a signal from the banking machine, he or she then inserts a deposit envelope. The computer records the deposit, but later someone must collect the envelope and verify the amount of money being deposited.

To protect itself from theft, the computer signals a camera to take two pictures of each person who tries to use the machine. If someone tries to break into the banking machine, the computer automatically alerts the police.

"Secret Computers" Answer

There are special-purpose computers inside:

the camera	the bathroom scale
the refrigerator	the sewing machine
the microwave oven	the dishwasher
the electronic game	the air-conditioner
the television	the stereo
the digital clock	the toy truck

Many new cars have hidden computers that regulate the flow of fuel to the engine for better mileage. Some, like the Cadillac Seville, also have special computer-controlled displays.

The computer-controlled climate panel shows the car's interior temperature and—at the touch of a button—records the outside temperature in degrees Fahrenheit (Celsius displays are available). Other displays provide the driver with information about the car's fuel level, speed, and fuel range in English and metric measurements.

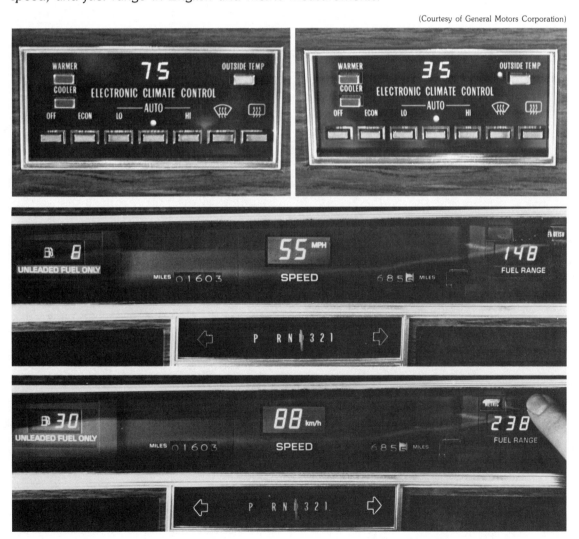

Just Following Orders

Computers are changing the world. Why, they've even given a new twist to crime. L. Benjamin Lewis, a Wells Fargo employee, discovered a flaw in the program directing the Wells Fargo Bank computer system. He used that loophole from late 1978 to early 1981 to steal twenty-one million dollars.

How did he do it? First, Lewis set up a phony organization, MAPS (Muhammad Ali Professional Sports), with a number of accounts at Wells Fargo branch banks. Then, as a MAPS board member, Lewis filled out a two-part form to transfer one hundred thousand dollars to a Beverly Hills branch account from a Santa Monica account. The Beverly Hills branch got the credit slip, but Lewis didn't send the withdrawal slip to the Santa Monica branch. There wasn't one hundred thousand dollars in the Santa Monica account. The computer system didn't catch the theft because it was set up to allow five days for the transfer process between branches. So, four days later, Lewis transferred an even larger phony sum from another branch to the Santa Monica account and then sent the withdrawal slip from the Beverly Hills transaction to the Santa Monica branch.

Lewis might have continued this money pyramid indefinitely if he hadn't slipped. He accidentally sent a withdrawal slip instead of a credit slip to the wrong branch bank. Wells Fargo quickly caught up with Lewis and took steps to make their computer program more sensitive to tampering. Crime had almost paid very well.

Blast! Pop! Gobble!

You lean toward the computer screen, gripping a <u>joystick</u> in each hand. A whole squad of alien spacecraft is zipping toward your rocket. You guide your craft to the left, blasting as you go.

You're in control of what's happening—right?

Wrong!

Video games are another type of special-purpose computer. You can only make choices that are built into the computer game's program.

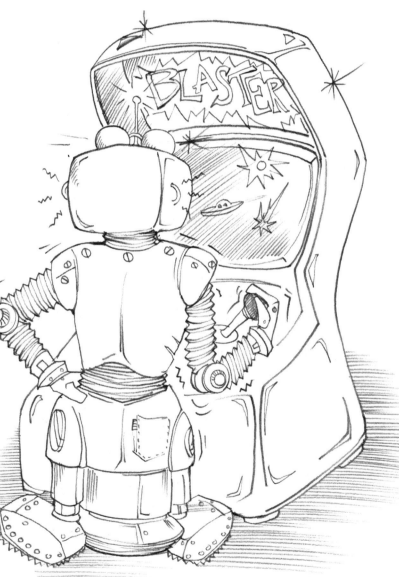

Do you love the yellow spot with the big mouth? Do you get a thrill out of watching the spot gobble up dots, apples, cherries, and strawberries? Do you giggle with delight when ghosts turn pale blue? Then you've got it. You've got "Pac-Man fever."

The Pac-Man game was designed several years ago by the Namco Corporation of Tokyo, Japan. Namco called it Paku Paku. This name means "snap, crackle, pop." It's the Japanese way of saying someone eats like a pig. The game was never very popular in Japan.

Output

JOYSTICK: a box with a knob that lets you control the movement of a lighted symbol on the screen.

But when Bally Midway Arcade Games brought Paku Paku to the U.S. and renamed it Pac-Man, the game became a big success. There were about 96,000 Pac-Man games and 108,000 Ms. Pac-Man games in arcades. Many more Pac-Man and Ms. Pac-Man games are now played at home on Atari systems.

Each arcade game gobbles an average of $200 in quarters each week. Two hundred dollars a week times 204,000 machines—Pac-Man is a game that eats money *paku paku*!

Part of the fun of playing Pac-Man is trying to top the high score of other players. Local machines only show local scores, but Bally is now sponsoring national competitions.

Who knows—one day, computer games may become an Olympic event. Maybe you will be the first to win a gold medal in this electronic competition.

Space Invaders Wrist and Pac-Man Elbow

These are the names doctors have given to physical problems caused by playing video games. Besides sore wrists and elbows, video-game players suffer from aching feet and strained eyes.

Maybe video games should carry a warning: BEWARE. This game can be dangerous to your health. (And it can leave you broke!)

I KEEP TELLING YOU, IT'S BYTE, NOT BITE!

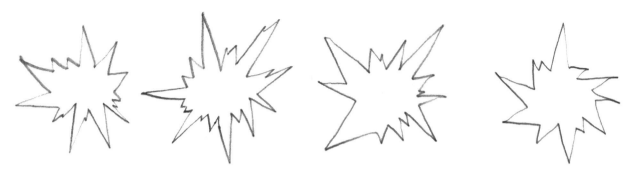

A Short, Short History of Video Games

Nolan Bushnell (founder of Atari) invented PONG in the early 1970's. That was the first successful video game. It used electronic paddles to slap a white blip back and forth across a television screen. It sold well for a few months. Then people became bored with the simple game.

There was little interest in video games until 1978, when the Taito Corporation of Japan introduced Space Invaders. This game had a changing skill level. As a player got better, the game became more difficult. Space Invaders also had sound effects.

Tunnel Two

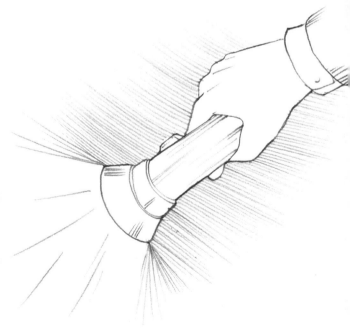

The tunnel curves to the right and then to the left. The passage becomes narrower and narrower. Finally you come to a rock wall. It's a dead end.

Your flashlight begins to blink. The batteries are getting weak.

Walking fast, you head back. You have to find your way out while you still have light.

(Hurry back to page 12 and try again.)

Space Invaders was an immediate success in Japan. Soon after the game was released, the Japanese treasury department was hit with a serious shortage of 100-yen coins. A little detective work located the missing coins. They were all in Space Invaders coin boxes.

Taito was flooded with demands for more games. To protect the games from theft, Taito Corporation had to make its deliveries at night in unmarked trucks.

Shortly after Space Invaders spread to the U.S. and Europe, Asteroids was released. It became popular because it was the first video game to add a feeling of competition by inviting players to record their initials and score.

Other games rushed to copy Space Invaders and Asteroids. In the U.S., video-game arcades began to open nationwide. But most of the games that filled the arcades lasted only a few months. Players quickly tired of the games and demanded new challenges.

In the early 1980's, Pac-Man and Ms. Pac-Man ate their way to the top. These became the first video games to remain popular for any length of time. And following Pac-Man's success, video games once more returned to the television screen. Only this time, the home video games were action-packed, colorful, and had super sound effects.

Meanwhile, arcade games were becoming more creative, and had started to talk. One by Sega growls, "So, a creature for my amusement," whenever a new player grabs the joystick.

And what will the future hold for video games? Probably more games will talk. Light and sound action will increase. Players may even be able to sit inside the video game to become involved in a three-dimensional fantasy world.

Only a few years old, these games are already a part of video-game history. In Japan most video games are called invader games because of the magnitude of Space Invaders' success.

Video Games Join the Army

The tank rolls into range. The M-2 troop transport fires. Ba-whoom! The tank on the screen explodes.

The soldier is practicing on an Atari game, using real controls and real firing equipment but no real tanks or live ammunition. Even at $3,500 a machine, the Atari game saves the army a bundle. Just one round of live ammunition for a tank costs $3,000.

Computer on Your Wrist

Watches used to be made with balance wheels, tiny springs, and gears. The gears moved back and forth to keep time.

Today's watches are operated by an electric current (supplied by a tiny battery) that vibrates inside a quartz crystal. The vibrating current passes through a special-purpose computer. The computer counts the vibrations to keep time.

A good watch made with springs and gears used to cost about a thousand dollars. It lost or gained at least two hours a year.

Today a good electronic quartz watch costs about a hundred dollars. It only loses or gains a minute a year.

Many watches with special-purpose computers also have built-in calculators, stopwatches, and alarm systems. Some include computer games—something to do while you're watching the clock.

(Courtesy of Seiko Time Corporation)

The "Sports 100" adjusts automatically to record the dates for odd and even months and provides time readings in three different time zones. As a stopwatch, it measures time accurately to a hundredth of a second.

More Hunting

You may have a computer on your wrist, in your pocket, or on your shelf right now. If you start looking, you'll find computers all around you, doing jobs that even Charles Babbage never dreamed of. See how many special-purpose computers you can track down in your neighborhood.

How can you tell there's a computer on the job?

76783   00350

Watch for computer codes. Black-line codes on packages are computer messages. A bar code reader can recognize the dark and light spaces. Then the computer lists the sale and checks to see whether it's time to restock that item.

Check different kinds of cards for a magnetic strip. If you find one on a credit card, a library card, or a bank card, a computer is getting the message.

Decide whether you are in complete control of the machines you use or whether you are only choosing from a limited number of choices. If you are getting to make only a few basic choices when you play the game, cook the food, or wash the clothes, a special-purpose computer is on the job.

You're the Boss

Special-purpose computers are designed to handle only one job. General-purpose computers can handle a lot of different jobs, and their programs can be changed easily. That means that you, the programmer, have lots of decisions to make about what jobs the computer will do. General-purpose computers are not hidden. A general-purpose computer may be in your classroom, in your parents' workplace, or in your own home. A basic unit looks something like this:

VIDEO SCREEN

KEYBOARD

General-purpose computers can keep track of airline reservations, process income-tax returns, and analyze information for medical research. They also can take care of the scheduling of students into various classes, plan and direct the assembly of parts in automobile manufacturing, and handle the accounting of a company's expenses and earnings. The same general-purpose computer can do all this and more, changing from one program to the next. In fact, the very largest general-purpose computers can have hundreds of people using them at the same time. Each person has his or her own terminal (keyboard and video screen, as shown), which is attached to the computer directly, through the telephone lines, or by satellite hookup. The computer handles all the different jobs so quickly that the people who use it are not aware that they are sharing the computer's time.

Computers Take Over the Movies

What would *Star Wars*, *The Empire Strikes Back*, and *Return of the Jedi* have been without a general-purpose computer? Dull!

The Industrial Light and Magic Company did the special effects for all of these George Lucas films using a computer-controlled camera. Called a flex camera, it was also special because it had such a wide range of movements. Attached to the end of a long metal arm, the camera could stretch up as high as eight feet and swing around on a forty-two-foot track. Controlled by a joystick, the flex camera could completely roll over. Think of those scenes where X-wing craft maneuvered in fantastic battles.

Each special-effect scene—one frame—was made up of many different pictures photographed one at a time. Then the individual pictures were layered into a film sandwich. Sometimes as many as thirty layers were needed to form one scene. Without the computer, the special effects could never have been pieced together in a perfect match.

First the camera angles and positions were planned. The computer stored that information during a test run. Then, as each part of the scene was shot, the computer sent the camera through the same sequence of moves. The results were *out of this world*.

Another Kind of Special Effect

In the Walt Disney movie *Tron,* many of the pictures were created entirely by a computer. First the ideas were drawn on paper, and these shapes were plotted on graph paper. Then a program was written to give the computer orders to draw each picture.

A computer screen is divided into rows and columns of dots or boxes. Each dot or box is a pixel—picture element. MAGI (Mathematical Applications Group, Inc.) made the pictures for *Tron* using a screen with more than two million pixels. The program told the computer which pixels to light, how bright to make them, and what color to make them appear.

When the pictures were exactly what the director wanted, the images were photographed. For *Tron,* even the background scenery was mostly computer-created. Of the 350 background scenes, 286 were computer-drawn.

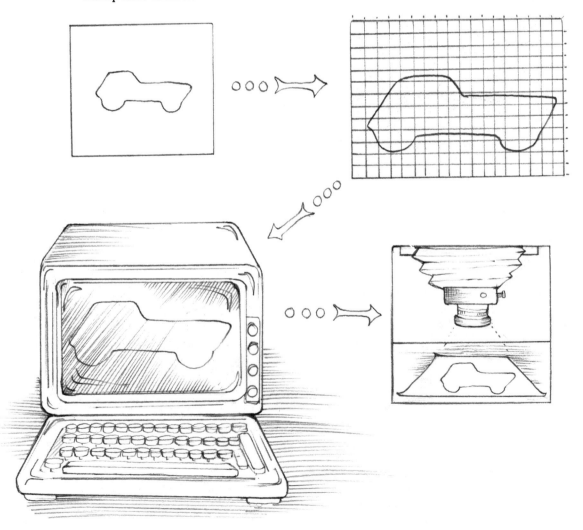

The Clever Thief

"James Colt is clever," Inspector McFee told FBI Agent Smith. "He used the bank's own computer system to gradually transfer more than a million dollars to his account. Taking out about ten thousand at a time, he withdrew half a million before the bank could catch him."

Smith nodded. "The new security program finally tracked down the theft."

"Yes, we got him," McFee agreed. "And we can prove he took the money. We just can't *find* the money."

"No idea where it could be?"

McFee frowned. "The worst part is that Colt only had fifteen minutes from the time he made his last withdrawal, twenty thousand dollars, until he was picked up. You can see for yourself that all Colt had in his pockets was some loose change. Where could he have hidden the money on Main Street in so short a time?"

"He's clever," Smith repeated, as he looked through the items that had been taken from James Colt's pockets. Then he smiled.

"But not clever enough. I know where the half-million is hidden."

Where is the money? How did Smith figure it out? If you don't know, the computer will give you a clue.

Special programs let you fill in the pixels on a computer screen with color to make designs or pictures. A paddle or joystick lets you move to the square you want to color. Pressing a number on the keyboard changes the pixel into the color of your choice.

To help you solve this caper, the computer has already coded the screen. Make a copy of this picture code on a piece of graph paper. Then use the key to color in the pixels.

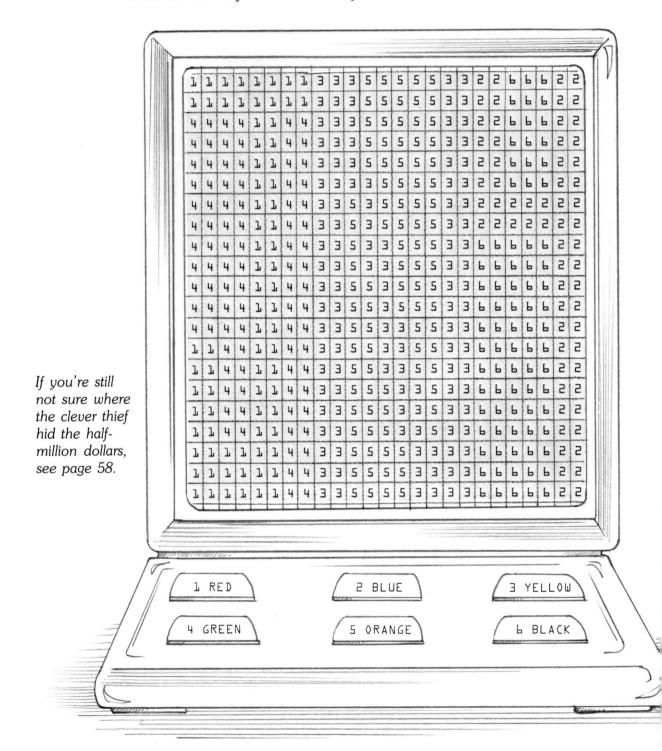

If you're still not sure where the clever thief hid the half-million dollars, see page 58.

Sounds Like the Real Thing

Before general-purpose computers went to work in the music industry, records were made the same way Thomas Edison had created the first ones. Sound waves were used to cut peaks and valleys into a record's grooved tracks.

When a needle made contact with the grooves, electrical impulses traveled to a speaker. The speaker made air waves vibrate, and the sounds were re-created.

This wasn't a bad way to make records, but it was impossible to capture all the details of the music with this method. Also, every time a record was played, a little of the groove was broken off and some more detail was lost.

In the system developed by the Sony and Philips corporations, sounds are translated into binary numbers—combinations of zeros and ones. A computer then stores this code on aluminum-plated disks. With this system, over 44,000 separate sound wavelengths per second can be recorded on a disk.

Instead of a needle, a tiny laser beam triggers the speakers to reproduce the sounds. With this method, music can be copied more exactly than ever before. The disks don't lose their quality. The music sounds like the original every time.

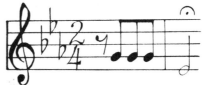

These are a few of the many thousands of numbers used by a computer to store the opening notes of Beethoven's Fifth Symphony.

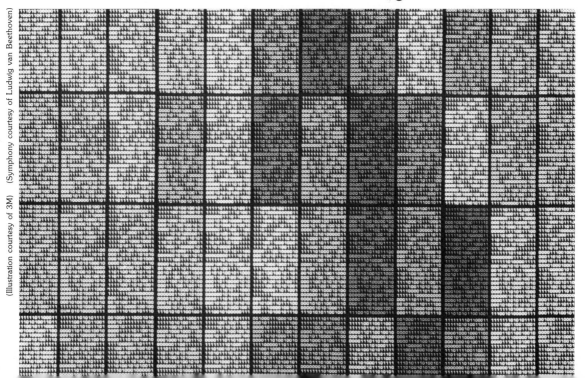

This cochlear prosthesis (artificial ear) is still being tested. The goal is to be able to implant it into the auditory nerve of someone who is profoundly deaf and have it pick up sounds, translate them into electrical impulses, and inject the impulses into the nerve in such a way that the sounds would be recognized by the brain.

Help for Humans

Computers can be small, lightweight, long-lasting, and low-energy users. That makes them perfect aids for humans who need help.

Artificial legs and arms are being made that move in response to sensors attached to the skin.

Computer-controlled pacemakers keep hearts beating.

The cochlear prosthesis uses a computer chip to change sound waves into electrical signals. These signals are sent directly to the brain's hearing center.

Such computer aids can't replace the body's normal functions, but they can make life better for many people.

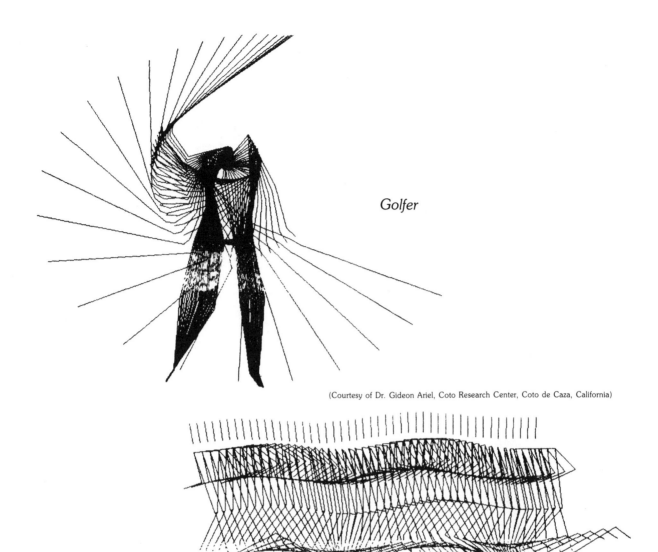

Golfer

(Courtesy of Dr. Gideon Ariel, Coto Research Center, Coto de Caza, California)

Runner

Computers can also help athletes improve their performance. First a high-speed film is made of the athlete in motion. Careful measurements are made of the athlete's body: arms, legs, chest. Heart rate is checked, breathing rate is recorded, and muscular strength is tested.

Next the film is projected onto a special screen in super-slow motion. The screen is like graph paper, with thousands of numbered squares. A wand is used to touch each square where the athlete's joints appear. This wand sends the information to a computer.

Comparing all the data, the computer displays a series of stick-figure shapes of the athlete's movements. The athlete is able to see any mistakes and wasted motions. After that it's up to the athlete to determine whether practice makes perfect.

"Clever Thief" Answer

A little checking by Smith turned up a rare-stamp and coin shop just down the street from the bank. Colt had arranged to purchase a block of four U.S. 24¢ airmail invert stamps valued at half a million dollars and had picked up the stamps the day he was caught. As part of his clever plan, Colt had hidden his prize stamps by sticking them on an envelope and stuffing the envelope into his pocket. Unfortunately for Colt, Agent Smith was also a stamp collector.

The story of the theft isn't true, but the stamps are real (and so is their value). The U.S. 24¢ airmail invert stamps are the result of a rare undiscovered printing error made by the U.S. Post Office in 1918.

Usually stamps that are not printed correctly are destroyed. But a block of one hundred stamps wasn't noticed until collector W. T. Robey purchased them on the day they were issued. The stamps show an upside-down Jenny (JN-4) airplane. Today, only ninety of the stamps are still known to exist. Only three or four blocks of four stamps are still together, making these blocks very valuable.

Do you see the mistake?

(Courtesy of Clifford C. Cole, Jr.)

What Computers Can't Do

Computers can't love, hate, worry, be afraid, or get tired. Computers can't judge right from wrong or have an opinion about something.

As you've discovered, this still leaves a lot of things that computers *can* be programmed to do. So how do computers handle all those jobs? The answer has to do with bits, bytes, memory, and a human programmer working with a well-engineered machine. How this machine works is what the next chapter is all about.

How Computers Work

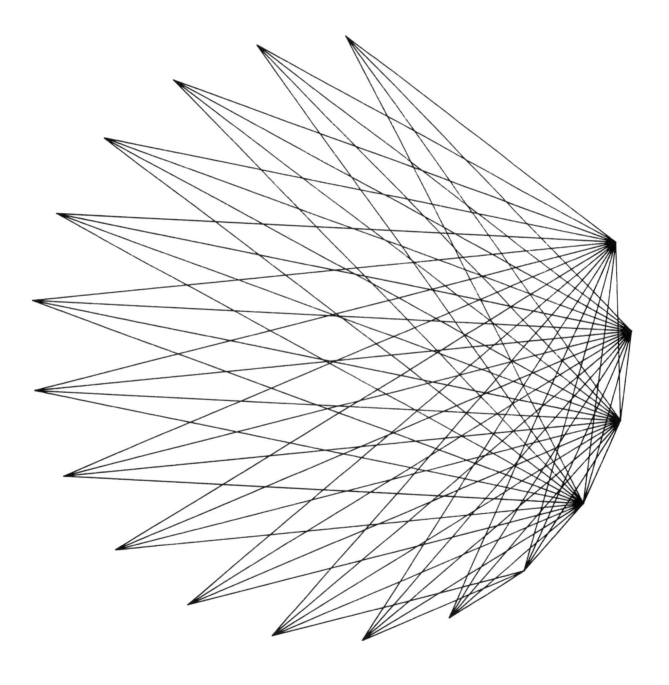

(Courtesy of Peachtree Software, Inc., an MSA Company)

Hardware

To perform its duties, a computer uses various types of equipment, called <u>hardware</u>. The main hardware consists of a keyboard, a Central Processing Unit, and a video screen.

<u>Input</u> is the term used to describe any information or orders, called <u>commands</u>, given to the computer. Most computer systems have a keyboard, which looks like a typewriter keyboard. The most common way to give a computer input is to type it in. Input can also be given through <u>disks</u>, magnetic tape, punched cards, or a light pen (when drawing models or designs). Some computers even understand spoken words.

The <u>Central Processing Unit</u> (CPU) is the circuitry inside the machine that <u>processes</u> and stores the <u>data</u>, or information, fed to the computer. With the right instructions, the Central Processing Unit can solve arithmetic problems, rearrange data, and test data.

Once the information is processed, it needs to be presented to you, the programmer, in a usable way. Computer responses are called <u>output</u>. The video screen, which looks like a television screen, is the most common way for a computer to give output. Output on paper is called a <u>printout</u>. Output may also be stored on disks, magnetic tape, or punched cards.

Any piece of hardware attached to the main body of the computer is called a peripheral—meaning "on the side." Some examples of these are:

a printer, which presents output in printed form

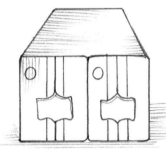

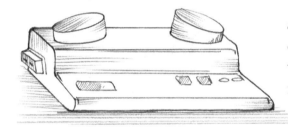

a disk drive, which spins the disk so information can be stored or made available to the computer

a modem, which hooks a computer to long distance phone lines. Then, when a connection is made with another computer, the two machines can quickly exchange information.

Other peripherals include a synthesizer and a plotter. A synthesizer changes electrical signals into music or voice-like speech. A plotter draws graphs, charts, and pictures.

Moving Around

A computer screen is like a big piece of graph paper. It is divided into columns and lines. On most computers, there is a TAB key or a combination of keys that can be pressed to perform the same function as the tabulator on a typewriter. The typewriter tab lets you jump ahead a certain number of spaces. The computer's TAB will let you leap to a new column on the right. You can't use it to go left.

As you move around, you will want to keep your eye on the cursor, a symbol that is always on a computer screen. It marks the next spot where a message will be presented or a symbol will appear if any key is pressed on the keyboard.

Software

The programs used on a computer are called software. You can write the programs yourself or use prepackaged ones written by others.

Programs are written in special computer languages that have been designed to allow you to communicate with the machine. Some of the many different computer languages are BASIC, FORTRAN, COBOL, Logo, and Pascal. BASIC (Beginner's All-purpose Symbolic Instruction Code) originally was designed to be used in education, but now it is also used in business and on home computers. It is probably the most frequently used computer language (and the one that will be used in this book). FORTRAN (Formula Translation) is used mainly in math and science research. COBOL (Common Business Oriented Language) is designed for writing reports and handling large amounts of data, and so it is used mostly in business. Logo (from the Greek word meaning "reason" and "logic") is designed for use in education and is oriented mainly toward the use of graphics. Pascal (named for Blaise Pascal) is designed to solve a lot of the problems that exist in computer languages developed earlier, as well as to make programming more efficient.

In the early days of working with computers, programmers had to work directly in binary code—zeros and ones. This code is called machine language, and it is the lowest-level language because it is closest to the "language" that the machine understands: the electrical *on* and *off* switches. Working in machine language did have an advantage. It allowed the programmer to have complete control of *every* job the machine performed. It was also very efficient. There were no wasted commands to take up storage space in the computer's memory circuits. Using machine language, however, required a lot of patience. It took time to change all data and instructions into machine language before feeding them to the computer as input. All output from the computer also had to be decoded. Another problem with using machine language was the similarity between number and letter codes. Look at the binary alphabet, called ASCII Code (American Standard for Information Interchange), in the box. This is one of several binary alphabets. Special instructions had to be included to clue the computer whether the code was for letters or numbers.

Eventually a language, called assembly language, was designed so that programmers could use code words instead of binary code. With assembly language, a special program, the assembler, handled the job of "reading" the coded program and changing it into machine language. Assembly language, an intermediate-level language, made working with the computer easier and faster for the programmer, but there were several disadvantages. Programmers no longer had complete control over the jobs the computer performed, since assembly

The Binary Alphabet					
A	0100 0001	J	0100 1010	S	0101 0011
B	0100 0010	K	0100 1011	T	0101 0100
C	0100 0011	L	0100 1100	U	0101 0101
D	0100 0100	M	0100 1101	V	0101 0110
E	0100 0101	N	0100 1110	W	0101 0111
F	0100 0110	O	0100 1111	X	0101 1000
G	0100 0111	P	0101 0000	Y	0101 1001
H	0100 1000	Q	0101 0001	Z	0101 1010
I	0100 1001	R	0101 0010		

language took them further away from machine language. And jobs were limited to the ones the assembler program could translate. In addition, assembly language was difficult enough to understand that experts were needed to handle the programming.

Through a continuing effort to make programming easier and faster, other code-reading programs were gradually developed along with their corresponding code languages. These are called high-level languages because they are furthest from the language that the computer "speaks" and "understands." High-level languages often use code words that are similar to English words, and they make programming simply a matter of choosing the right command functions that are available in a certain language. However, with high-level languages, the programmer has even less control over the jobs the computer handles and the program that translates the high-level language into machine language (the compiler or the interpreter) takes up space in the computer's memory circuits while it's compiling.

Compiler programs are generally run only after the entire program has been entered in code language. When it has finished grinding through its job of translating, the compiler lists all errors that need correction. FORTRAN is an example of a compiled language.

Interpretive languages translate commands one at a time as they are entered or as they are read from memory, and the programmer is notified of errors as they occur. BASIC is an example of an interpretive language. Most interpretive languages also have compiled versions. The advantage of using an interpreter is that the program runs immediately so that the programmer can keep making changes until the job is done to his or her satisfaction. With a compiler, a number of steps are required before the program goes into action, which makes revising a slower process. A compiled program, however, is more efficient, takes up less space in the computer's memory circuits, and runs faster.

The next step beyond high-level languages may be automatic program generators. For these, the computer will ask questions (possibly even in spoken words) about the kind of job the programmer wants done. Then the computer will create a program to perform that task. The programmer may not even need to understand much about how a computer works.

Tunnel Three

As you are walking down the tunnel, you hear a distant rumble. Thunder? Maybe you are getting close to the surface.

The rumbling grows louder. You walk faster. Dust and pebbles begin to rain on you from the tunnel ceiling. Small rocks pelt your head and shoulders. The tunnel is caving in.

You turn and run as fast as you can back to the cavelike room. Panting and brushing off the dust, you choose another tunnel.

(Go back to page 12 and pick a new direction.)

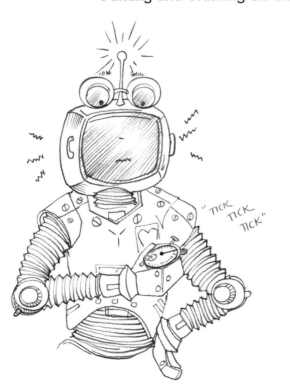

"TICK TICK TICK"

Mini-Mystery

Ohio is a four-letter word with three vowels. What is another state whose name contains four letters, three of which are vowels? With the right data and instructions, a computer can display the answer to this mystery in less than a second. Time yourself on this one.

(See page 94.)

A Bit of Magic

"And now," announced the magician, "I'll make myself disappear."

As the crowd watched, the magician whirled around. There was a puff of smoke, and the magician was gone. In the magician's place there was a computer displaying three riddles. But the magician's magic had also affected the machine. All of the answers to the riddles were displayed in machine language.

To find out where the magician went, you'll need to decode the riddle answers using the binary alphabet on page 63. Then unscramble the circled letters. (See page 77.)

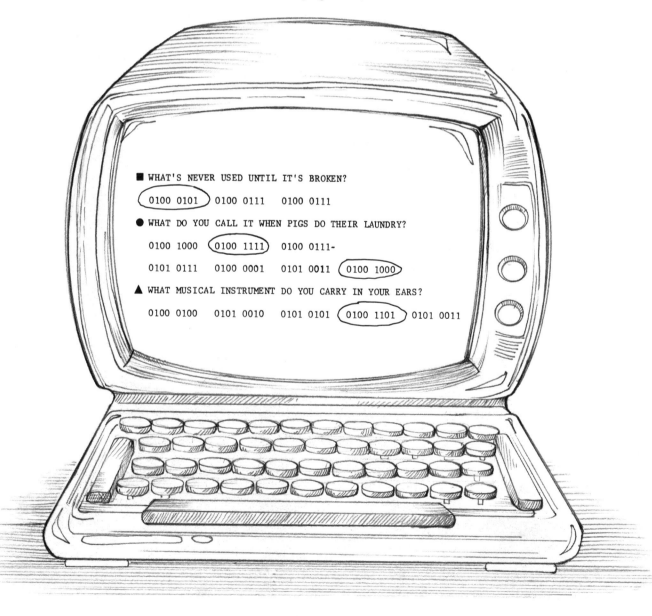

■ WHAT'S NEVER USED UNTIL IT'S BROKEN?

(0100 0101) 0100 0111   0100 0111

● WHAT DO YOU CALL IT WHEN PIGS DO THEIR LAUNDRY?

0100 1000 (0100 1111) 0100 0111-

0101 0111   0100 0001   0101 0011 (0100 1000)

▲ WHAT MUSICAL INSTRUMENT DO YOU CARRY IN YOUR EARS?

0100 0100   0101 0010   0101 0101 (0100 1101) 0101 0011

Memory

There are some things, such as writing your name or tying your shoes, that you do so often that they seem to be a permanent part of your memory. Other things, such as the rules to a game, may be easy to remember while you're using them, but you soon forget them afterward. And finally, there's a set of memories that can be called up if you work at remembering. What was your first-grade teacher's name? That's okay—give it a minute. It will come to you.

Computers also have three memory systems to help them store data and programs.

<u>ROM</u> is <u>read-only memory</u>. ROM is burned into the computer's circuits. In a special-purpose computer, the instructions for all the jobs it does may be in ROM. In a general-purpose computer, read-only memory usually contains only the instructions for activating the <u>Operating System</u> (OS). This, then, is the first job a general-purpose computer does when it is switched on. The Operating System is a computer's master control program. Like a traffic controller, it directs bringing other programs into the computer's circuits, moving data, and processing data.

<u>Internal memory</u>, sometimes called <u>RAM (random-access memory)</u> is in the CPU's circuits. As long as electricity is flowing through the computer's chips, bits can be *on* or *off*—one or zero. When the electricity stops flowing, the information stored in the chips is erased.

Mini-Mystery

This is the way movie star Linda Carson's jewelry box looked before she was robbed.

"Oh, dear," Linda Carson sighed. "I just don't know what is missing."

How good is your memory? Look at the picture for thirty seconds. Then look at the picture of the jewelry box after the robbery (page 74).

Can you tell what is missing?

Besides being stored in a computer's circuits, programs and data can be stored on peripheral equipment, such as floppy disks, cassette tapes, or reels of tape. The stored information and programs are available to the computer through a disk drive, a cassette tape player, or a reel-to-reel tape player. The computer can't process this external memory as quickly as what's stored in its own circuits. But there is an advantage to external memory. When the electricity is off, data and programs stored in external memory are still there.

Needs TLC (Tender, Loving Care)

Floppy disks are a lot like soft records. Information and orders are recorded on the disks in binary code. The code shows up as magnetic patterns on circular tracks. The tracks are a lot like the ridges on a real phonograph record.

Disks will last a long time, but they need special care. Never write on a disk's jacket with a ball-point pen. The pressure will ruin the coded pattern. Disks also can't stand to be hot, wet, or dusty.

A Computer of Your Own

You can explore how a computer works by building a model. To do this, you'll need:

one large empty cereal box
one smaller empty cereal box
one shoe box
eighty inches of rope (twine, string, or yarn can be used)
a piece of white poster board, 22 inches wide and 28 inches long
a roll of adding-machine tape
scissors
glue
felt-tip pen

(For a more professional-looking model, you may want to cut construction paper and glue it over the sides of the boxes to cover the print before you begin.)

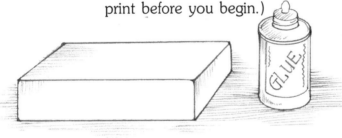

There are a number of different keyboard arrangements and types of keys. Your model's keyboard is not a real one, but includes all the main keyboard features.

To make the keyboard, cut a piece of poster board to cover one side of the smaller cereal box. Use the felt-tip pen to copy the computer keyboard shown below on the poster board. Then glue the keyboard onto the box.

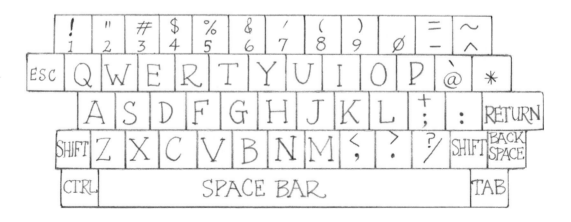

The Computer's IQ = K

A computer's "intelligence" depends on how many bytes of information can be stored in its memory. K stands for 1,024. A computer with 64K memory can store 65,536 bytes of eight bits each.

To make the video screen, set the larger cereal box on edge lengthwise, as shown, in a horizontal position. On the side facing you, cut two pairs of slits about two inches long and five inches apart. Thread the adding-machine tape through these slits, as shown.

The tape between the slits is your model's video screen. When it is pulled past the box, it becomes the printout. The adding-machine paper shows output from your computer.

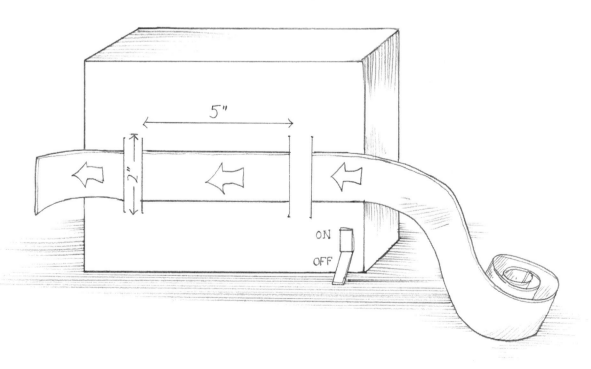

Cut a small tab from the poster board and crease it firmly in the center. Glue one half of this piece to the larger cereal box, as shown on page 71. Write *on* and *off* near each end of the tab. This is your computer's electrical switch. A computer can't do anything without electricity moving through its circuits.

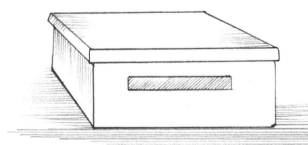

To make the Central Processing Unit, cut out three poster-board pieces about one-half inch square. Glue these together, as shown. These three pieces are the computer's integrated-circuit chips. The center chip is the microprocessor—the control center for the computer. The add-on chips give the computer extra memory. Together they form the Central Processing Unit. Set these aside for the moment.

On one long side of the shoe box, cut a narrow slot, as shown. The box is your model's disk drive.

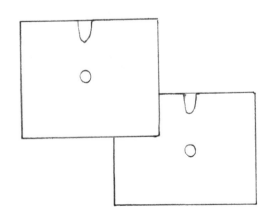

Now cut two square floppy disks from poster board. Make them small enough to fit through the slot. Cut out a center circle and draw on a slot, as shown. Set these aside with your poster-board chips.

Finally, cut two pieces of rope, each about twenty-four inches long. Cut holes in the three boxes just large enough to poke the rope through. Knot the rope pieces inside the boxes so they won't pull out.

The ropes are the electrical cords that connect the parts of your computer system. To the side or back of the large cereal box, attach another piece of rope knotted on the inside. This is your computer's power cord. Now your system has everything but memory.

Print BRING IN OS on your poster-board chips and put these into the large cereal box. This gives your computer its Central Processing Unit, complete with the ROM memory it needs to get started as well as the circuitry for its internal memory. This means your computer's CPU has the permanent memory to bring in the Operating System program from storage the moment it is turned on, along with the capability of storing internal-memory information in its circuits.

Starting up a computer is called <u>booting</u>. To boot yours, pretend to plug it in (never really put anything into an electrical outlet). Flip on the switch and put the poster-board disks into the disk drive. The disks form your computer's external memory.

One disk contains the Operating System to direct and control operations and a compiler or an interpreter to act as a translator between you and your computer. You can pretend to use the other disk for storing the programs you write. You'll learn how to store programs in the next chapter, "Writing Programs," but for now, you'll just want to use internal memory as you experiment with giving orders to your computer.

Mini-Mystery Answer

The robber took: the barrette, the leaf pin, the heart, the coin, the diamond ring, the pearl necklace, the gold chain, the gold band, the eagle pin, and the watch. A computer could store a detailed description of this jewelry and a lot more to list on command.

ZRTWCDAEOKJGS

All Caps

Early computers displayed only capital letters. This became traditional and was used even though computers were capable of displaying upper and lowercase letters. Now the trend is to make computers display both. Research has proven that a mix of capital and lowercase letters is easier to read.

Big Pocket Calculator

Type <u>PRINT</u> on your model computer's keyboard. Then type 42 − 17. (BASIC uses these symbols for math problems: + for addition, − for subtraction, * for multiplication, and / for division.) Typing on the computer keyboard is just like typing on a typewriter. Touch the space bar each time you want to space. A real computer's video screen would show what you had typed. So write PRINT 42 − 17 on your model's screen.

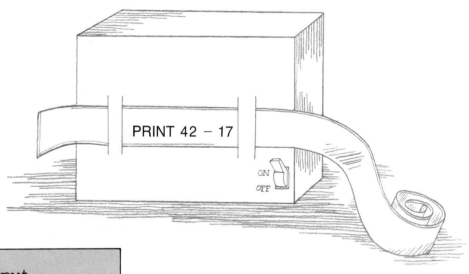

Output

PRINT: BASIC command telling the computer to display what follows it.

You have just given your model computer a short program—a one-liner. Now press the key labeled <u>RETURN</u> (on some computers it is labeled ENTER). When this key is pressed, the information you have typed is sent to the computer's CPU. If, as in this case, a response from the computer is ordered by the statement, the computer will show that response on the next line. On a real computer, the answer to 42 − 17 would be displayed on the video screen directly below the problem. So write 25 below 42 − 17.

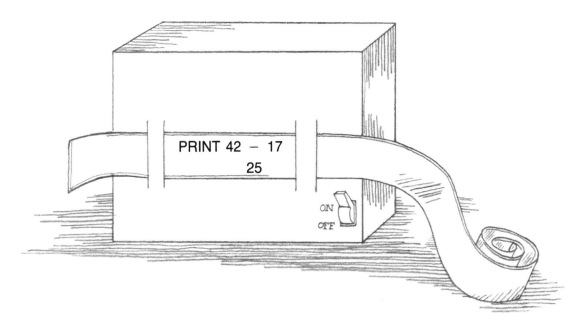

When you slide the adding-machine tape past the screen, the program and response become a printout. In a real system, a printed message would be produced by a printer.

CAN I QUOTE YOU?

SURE, JUST HOLD DOWN SHIFT KEY, AND PRESS KEY MARKED "2

PRESS

PRESS PASS

"Bit of Magic" Answer

■ EGG
● HOGWASH
▲ DRUMS

The magician went HOME.

You Can Quote Me

The PRINT command can also be used to make the computer display a readable message. To do this, however, the computer needs to be signaled as to what to store and display.

The quotation marks (") are the BASIC symbol that clues the computer to store and display the letters, numbers, or symbols that follow. While some computers use other combinations of keys, to send *your* computer the quotation-mark code, hold down the SHIFT key while you press the key marked "2. This will make only the quotation marks appear on the screen.

Now you're ready to try having your computer quote you. Type PRINT. Hold down the SHIFT key while you press "2. Then type SMILE I LIKE YOU and another set of quotation marks. When you press the RETURN key, the computer will display everything that was stored between the two sets of quotation marks: SMILE I LIKE YOU. The computer does not show the " at the beginning and end of its response. Now make up a message of your own for the computer to quote. Run your message program on your model or on a real computer.

What Would the Computer Say?

Give each of these commands to your model computer. Pick which response the computer would give and show it on the model's screen. Then check yourself on a real computer or on page 84.

■ PRINT 4 * 2................	SYNTAX ERROR	"8"	8
● PRINT HI BOSS............	SYNTAX ERROR	0	HI BOSS
▲ PRINT "63 / 7"............	SYNTAX ERROR	9	63 / 7
(PRONT "YOU ARE NICE".....	SYNTAX ERROR	0	YOU ARE NICE

Getting the Message

Nobody's perfect. So what if you make a mistake in how you spell PRINT? The computer will still understand what you want done—won't it?

No! PRINT, remember, is a BASIC code word. It must be spelled correctly to call up the right list of orders in assembly language. If you misspell PRINT or any other command code word, the computer displays: <u>SYNTAX ERROR</u>. This means that the computer did not receive your order. You'll have to try again.

If you misspell a word after you type the quotation-mark code, the computer will store and display your mistake. It's just quoting you.

If you omit the quotation marks when you want the computer to display a message, the computer responds: 0. (Without the ", the computer stores the words after the PRINT command as the number 0.)

Zero

Most computers show zero as 0. This is because when they print capital letters zero would look like capital letter O without the slash.

Mini-Mystery Answer

$58 + 62 = \underline{120} / 6 = \underline{20}$
$* 4 = \underline{80} = 5 = \underline{85}$
$- 3 = \underline{82} / 2 = \underline{41}$
$+ 59 = \underline{100}$

(See page 97.)

Mainframes, Minis, and Micros

There are three main groups of computers. Mainframes are the biggest. Because of the amount of internal circuitry they have, mainframes can handle and process data more quickly than minis or micros. They can have more peripherals (disk drives, modems, printers) under their control. A mainframe can handle many different jobs at the same time.

Mainframes are very expensive. They are used by big businesses and government agencies. A mainframe in a central office can process and store data from many branch offices.

Minis are smaller, store less data, and work more slowly than mainframes. Minis are able to handle more than one job at a time. Their abilities are best suited for local companies that don't need to handle a lot of business over telephone lines. They are less expensive than mainframes.

Micros are personal home computers and small one-office computers. They are very inexpensive compared to minis and mainframes. But their memory can only handle one job at a time.

It's okay to use a computer the way you would use a pocket calculator or a message printer. But a computer can do a lot more. Bigger jobs, though, mean bigger programs. Are you ready for bigger challenges? Well, then, don't wait another minute to turn the page and get started.

Writing Programs

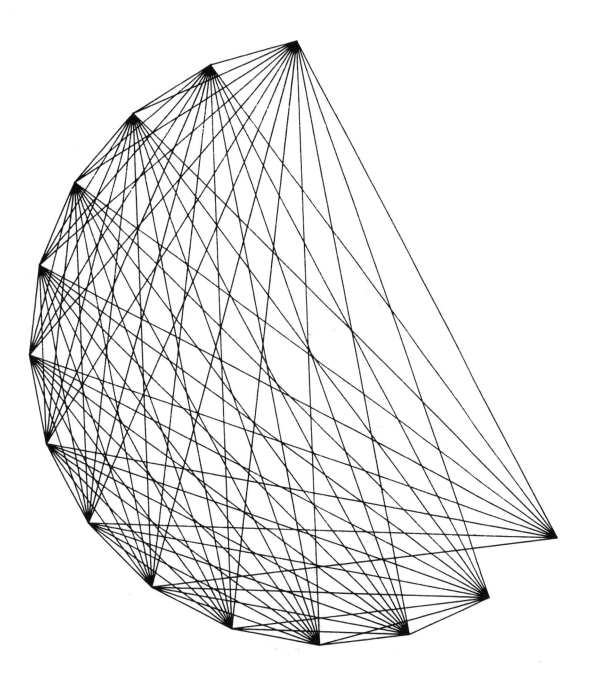

(Courtesy of Peachtree Software, Inc., an MSA Company)

Giving Orders

Your mom says, "Sure. You can have some popcorn, but you'll have to make it yourself."

Okay. No problem. You can handle the job without any other instructions. You can, but a computer-run robot couldn't.

As the boss of a robot, you would have to plan the job, prepare a detailed set of orders, and organize any decision-making situations so that the computer-run robot could handle them. This is because:

A computer can only do what you tell it to do.
A computer needs to be told how to do each part of the job.
A computer has to be given orders on how to handle
any problems that might come up.

Sound like a lot of work? It is. But once you do the planning and write the program, the computer-run robot can handle the job again and again.

Giving Enough Orders

When you write a program for a computer, you have to include orders for every part of the job. Anything you forget to tell the computer to do will not be done.

This list of instructions tells a computer-run robot how to make popcorn. It isn't complete.

Get out a pan.
Get out a tablespoon.
Put two tablespoons of oil in the pan.
Turn the burner on to medium-high.
Get out the popcorn.
Pour enough corn into the pan to cover the bottom.
Listen for the corn to pop.
When the corn stops popping, take the pan from the stove.
Turn off the burner.

More Orders

Put the pan on a burner on the stove.
Get out the oil.
Open the popcorn container.
Put a lid on the pan.

Look at the "More Orders" box. Decide where each order in the box should be added to the instruction list. Is the program complete? Does it, for example, tell the robot to add melted butter or salt to the popcorn? And what about cleaning up the kitchen?

Now try to do something (tie your shoes, draw a picture, make a sandwich) while a friend tells you exactly what to do. You're the computer-run robot. Don't do anything without an order. Then try programming your friend to perform a task.

When Is Important

Just planning each step that a computer-run robot will do isn't enough. As you probably discovered while you were pretending to be a robot, *when* you get an order is also important.

What if the robot was told to turn off the stove before the corn stopped popping? What would happen?

What if the robot was not told to put the lid on the pan until after the corn stopped popping? What would happen?

"What Would the Computer Say?" Answer

■ 8   ● 0   ▲ 63 / 7   (SYNTAX ERROR

Decisions . . . Decisions

You can be asked to make very general kinds of decisions. What did you think of the movie? How are you planning to earn money for a new bike?

Computers can only make decisions that involve a choice between two specific things. And a computer's choices are always made in mathematical terms. Is A more than B? Is 9 less than 2? Is car equal to automobile? Is noon not equal to midnight? Many computers use these symbols for decision-making.

More than >	Equal to =
Less than <	Not equal to < >

Spot Check

A computer could be asked to decide whether each of these statements is *true* or *false*. What's your decision?

■ 10 > 75
● Night < > Day
▲ A < Z
★ Ice = Ice
(7 > 8
□ 1 < 12

▲ True   □ True
● True   ) False
■ False   ★ True

Mini-Mystery

Using scissors, how can you cut a paper circle into eight pieces with just three cuts?

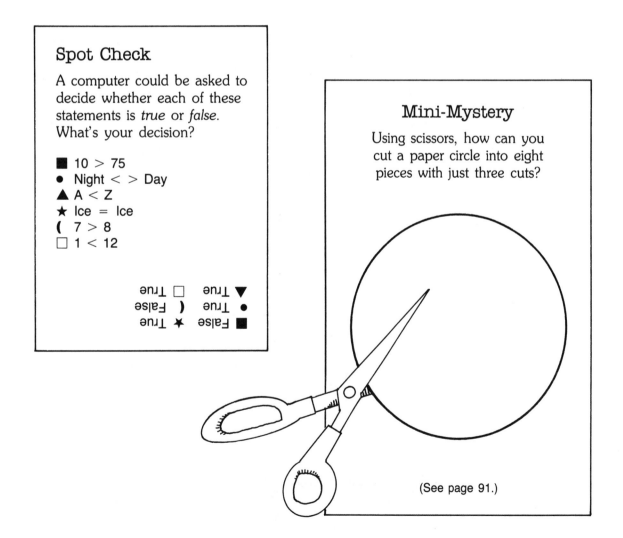

(See page 91.)

Flowing Along

Because programs that are longer than one-liners take careful planning, programmers use <u>flowcharts</u> to help them. Flowcharts are diagrams that show each step of the program in the order in which it needs to be done. Special shapes are used to show what kind of operation the computer will need to perform at each step.

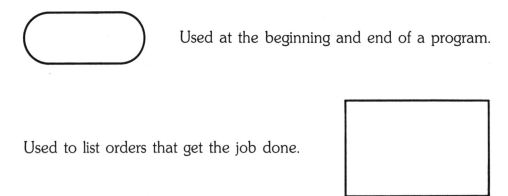

Used at the beginning and end of a program.

Used to list orders that get the job done.

Used to show a point where the computer will have to make a decision. It marks a branch in the program.

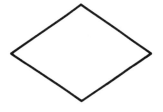

Used to record information that will be given as input and stored by the computer to be used in the program.

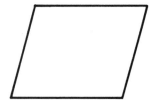

Shows the direction to follow through the program.

Mystery Number (A Computer Game)

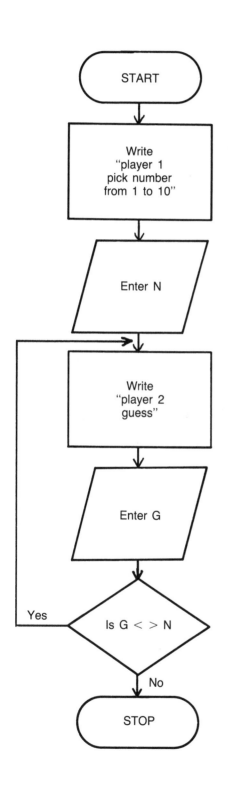

This flowchart is a plan for a number-guessing game. Player 1 will pick a number (N) from one to ten and type it in, following the computer command, to be stored in the computer's memory. This is the mystery number.

Once N is entered, the computer will display: PLAYER 2 GUESS. And player 2 will have a chance to enter a guess (G). The computer will then compare the guessed number to the stored mystery number. If the numbers are not equal, the computer will go back through the guessing step. If the numbers match, the program is finished.

Mini-Mystery

What is twice one half of 1,000,000?

(See page 95.)

Tunnel Four

As you are walking along the tunnel, your flashlight goes out. You shake it, but it won't come back on. The batteries are dead.

You keep walking—slowly. You stretch out your arms. It is completely dark. You can't see anything.

Suddenly the wall stops. You lean forward, trying to feel your way. You slip. Down, down you tumble.

Whomp!

You land on a hard dirt floor. There is something behind you.

It's a box. You tug the lid open. You can feel coins. You can hear them rattle and clink.

A beam of sunlight slices through the darkness, glinting on the coins, and you blink in the light. "Gold!" you say. Then you jerk your head up.

You're at the bottom of an old well. The light is coming through a crack in the wooden hatch that covers the well.

There is just enough light for you to find toeholds and fingerholds in the old stone walls of the well. You stuff gold coins into your pockets and climb up. One push is enough to shove off the rotten hatch. You crawl out onto the ground.

You've found the treasure. And you've *escaped*!

You run for help before Peterson and McThug can find you.

From Flowchart to Program

Moving from a flowchart to a program that will make the computer do the job requires using code words and giving orders in a special way.

Each statement (one command or a group of commands that go together) begins when you type in a <u>line number</u>. This clues the computer that commands are coming and sets up the order in which the individual tasks are to be done. Line numbers usually go up by tens to leave space for adding other statements later.

A code word always follows the line number to tell the computer what kind of task it will be performing. Then comes the information—what needs to be done. The line number and the statement appear on the screen as you type them in.

Bill NONE

In 1977 Skip Swenson of Los Angeles, California, chose NONE for the lettering on his license plate. A few weeks later Skip got a bill for $953 worth of unpaid parking tickets.

Skip was not guilty of a lot of illegal parking. The police had a habit of writing NONE in the license blank any time an illegally parked car had no tag. The computer simply totaled the unpaid fines and sent the bill to Skip.

NOW I DON'T HAVE TO FLY AROUND LOOKING FOR MY FAVORITE BLOOD TYPE!

YUM...

Output

INPUT: BASIC command to make the computer ask for a response. If the program asks for one answer and you give more than one, the computer displays:

EXTRA IGNORED

The computer only processes your first answer.

END: BASIC command that signals the end of processing.

Mystery Number Programmed

Here's the program for Mystery Number. Think about the ways that the program is different from the flowchart. Then read what is happening inside the computer at each step.

Program	Inside the Computer
NEW	Fast-memory circuits are cleared.
10 PRINT "PLAYER 1 PICK A NUMBER FROM 1 TO 10"	Message is stored as well as displayed during processing.
20 INPUT N	INPUT is a BASIC command that makes the computer display a question mark (?). The program user can then type in a response that will be stored for use during processing.

30 PRINT "PLAYER 2 GUESS"	Message is stored as well as displayed during processing.
40 INPUT G	During processing, question mark will be displayed and typed-in response will be stored.
50 IF G < > N THEN GOTO 30	G is compared to N. No match sends the computer back to line 30. IF . . . THEN . . . GOTO are commands that set up a loop, a way to repeat part of a program. Loops are explored further in the chapter called "Tricks of the Trade."
60 PRINT "YOU GUESSED IT"	Message stored for display when G = N.
70 END	Signals the end of processing.

Mini-Mystery Answer

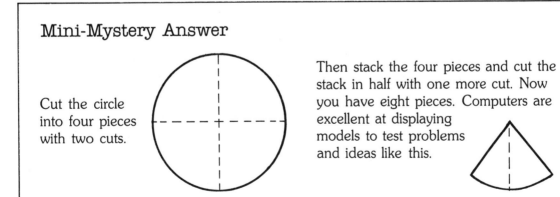

Cut the circle into four pieces with two cuts.

Then stack the four pieces and cut the stack in half with one more cut. Now you have eight pieces. Computers are excellent at displaying models to test problems and ideas like this.

General Housekeeping Commands

Some commands don't need to follow a line number. These general BASIC commands take care of tidying up the screen, clearing out fast memory, and putting programs into action.

NEW erases anything being stored in fast memory. It signals the computer to get ready to store new data and instructions.

HOME is the command that moves the cursor back to its starting position in the upper left corner and clears the screen on the Apple. Your computer probably has a similar command.

RUN tells the computer to search through its memory for a program. If this command is used immediately following a program's entry, the computer finds the beginning and then follows the commands after each line number one at a time. If RUN is used with the code name for a particular program, the computer searches its external memory for the program. Then it follows the instructions.

DIRECTORY can be used to show you what programs you have stored on your floppy disk. Like a menu in a restaurant, this BASIC command displays the code names of all the programs that are available. On some computer systems the command that serves up the menu may be CATALOG or FILES. However, the computer only stores BASIC program names as eight characters. For longer titles, therefore, a programmer has to abbreviate and run words together (Mstrynum for Mystery Number, for example). For titles shorter than eight characters, the computer will display spaces after the name to make up the difference. When the computer displays the names, it will also display · BAS after each, to let the programmer know the code language used in these programs is BASIC.

SUPRSTAR	· BAS	HELLO	· BAS
TAXPACK	· BAS	COLORWAR	· BAS
CHASE	· BAS	MSTRYNUM	· BAS
POKER	· BAS	FATCAT	· BAS

To see one of these programs, you would type RUN and the program's name. You may need to type quotes around the program's title (check your computer's instructions). Then press the RETURN key.

LIST is another command that doesn't need a line number. It allows a programmer to look at a program or a part of a program. If the computer has just performed its duties and you would like another look at the program, type LIST. The statements that make up the program will appear on the screen. Other housekeeping commands, such as NEW and HOME, will not be displayed.

```
      NEW
10  PRINT "SNAP"
20  PRINT "CRACKLE"
30  PRINT "AND POP"
40  END
```

Enter this program on your model computer. Then type LIST 20 and press the RETURN key. The computer will display just the part you ordered delivered. So on your computer's screen show: 20 PRINT "CRACKLE".

Fix It or Throw It Out

```
    NEW
10  PRINT "WHAT HAS HANDS BUT CAN'T SCRATCH ITSELF?"
20  PRINT "I DON'T KNOW"
30  PRONT "A CLOCK"
40  END
```

Programmers refer to problems that keep a program from working as <u>bugs</u>. Do you see the bug in this program?

When you type RUN, the computer will display: SYNTAX ERROR. That, remember, is the computer's way of signaling you that the problem is a mistake with one of the command code words. You'll need to type LIST to make the computer display the program again. Do you see which line has the bug now?

You don't have to retype the whole program to fix it. Just retype the line that you want to change: 30 PRINT "A CLOCK". When you press the RETURN key the corrected line will be stored in place of the incorrect one.

If you would like to get rid of line 20, first type LIST to have the program displayed. Then type 20, but don't type what follows the number. When you press the RETURN key the computer will remove line 20 from the program.

It is possible to make these program changes because line numbers assign a definite location in the computer's circuits for instructions or data to be stored. Each time that location is assigned a new statement, the old one is erased. Being able to correct or erase lines without retyping the whole program is particularly useful with very long programs.

Spot Check

```
    NEW
10  PRINT "HELLO"
20  PRINT "HOW ARE YOU?"
30  END
```

What command do you need to make the computer process this program?

You need to type RUN.

Mini-Mystery Answer
Iowa

YES, I'M SURE. FLYPAPER WON'T KEEP THE BUGS OUT.

Output

= : BASIC symbol that
tells the computer to
replace (store) data at
a coded location.

For Safekeeping

Another way to store information in a computer's memory is to use variables. The term <u>variable</u> means the process of giving numbers or words a code name and allowing the computer to handle finding a location in its circuits to store that information.

For a number, initializing the variable (giving it a code name) is done by stating that the code name equals (=) the number.

```
NEW
10   A = 7
20   PRINT A
30   END
```

If you typed RUN for the above program and pressed the RETURN key, the computer would then search its memory for A and print what was stored at that coded location.

```
NEW
10   X = 4
20   PRINT X
30   X = X * 3
40   PRINT X
50   X = X + 6
60   PRINT X
70   END
```

When performing the duties of the program on the left, the computer would search for X each time it reached PRINT X, and it would display that stored number. Each time X is said to equal a new value (lines 30 and 50), the computer erases what is stored at the location coded X and replaces it with the new information.

Stringing Along

Variables that store words are called <u>string variables</u> because of the way storage circuits may be strung together in the computer's memory. Numbers always take up the same amount of storage space in memory. The code changes, but the number of bytes is unaffected. There is no additive way to form words, and so putting letters together requires more storage space. Look at the difference in binary translation between adding 10 to 1 and adding ILL to B:

```
10  A = 1 (0000 0001)        10  T$ = "B" (0100 0010)
20  PRINT A                  20  PRINT T$
30  A = A + 10               30  T$ = T$ + "ILL"
40  PRINT A (0000 1011)      40  PRINT T$ (0100 0010 0100 1001
                                 0100 1100 0100 1100)
```

A string variable's code name always ends in a dollar sign ($). A number variable's name can't have a $.

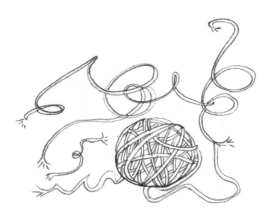

Output

$: BASIC symbol that tells the computer to store words.

+ : BASIC symbol used to string any kind of data together.
```
Q = C + D + 5
Q$ = C$ + D$ + "SMILE"
```

An Arm in Space

Space Shuttle astronauts have a giant robot arm to move objects out of the cargo bay while in orbit. This fifty-foot jointed arm was designed by a Canadian company and has its actions controlled mainly by a computer. But the arm's designers left one important control job to the astronauts: a collision-avoidance system would have taken up a lot of precious computer memory, so the astronauts have to watch over the arm while it works to prevent it from shoving heavy payloads through the orbiter's walls.

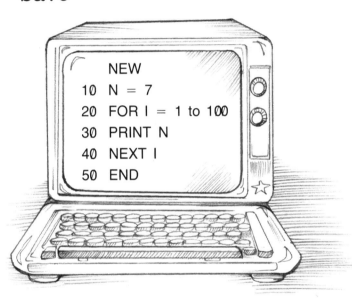

Mini-Mystery Answer

A computer can test any number arrangement quickly to solve such a program, or it can generate a puzzle like this one to challenge the user.

7	6	11
12	8	4
5	10	9

Save

```
      NEW
10    N = 7
20    FOR I = 1 to 100
30    PRINT N
40    NEXT I
50    END
```

Is seven your lucky number? Well, this program will display 100 sevens. You can run this program anytime you want by sending it from fast memory to external memory for safekeeping. To store the program on a disk, first give the program a code name—Lucky 7.

Then type: SAVE "LUCKY 7". The next time you want to see a whole lot of sevens, type: LOAD "LUCKY 7".

You can either LIST to see the program displayed or RUN to put it into action.

Output

SAVE: BASIC command that tells a computer to move a program from internal memory to external memory.

LOAD: BASIC command that tells the computer to move a program from external memory to internal memory.

Save It on Tape

Some computers use tape recorders and cassette tapes rather than disk drives or disks. This form of storage is much cheaper but offers less storage space. Usually only one program is stored on each cassette. So use the short ten-minute cassettes.

1. Rewind the tape.
2. Type: SAVE. (No code name is needed.)
3. Push *record* and then *play* to start the tape recorder.
4. Press the RETURN key to start the computer and send the program to the tape recorder.

Lucky 7 uses a neat programming trick. To find out about this, plus ways to make programs shorter, easier to write, and full of pizzazz, don't miss "Tricks of the Trade." It's next.

Tricks of the Trade

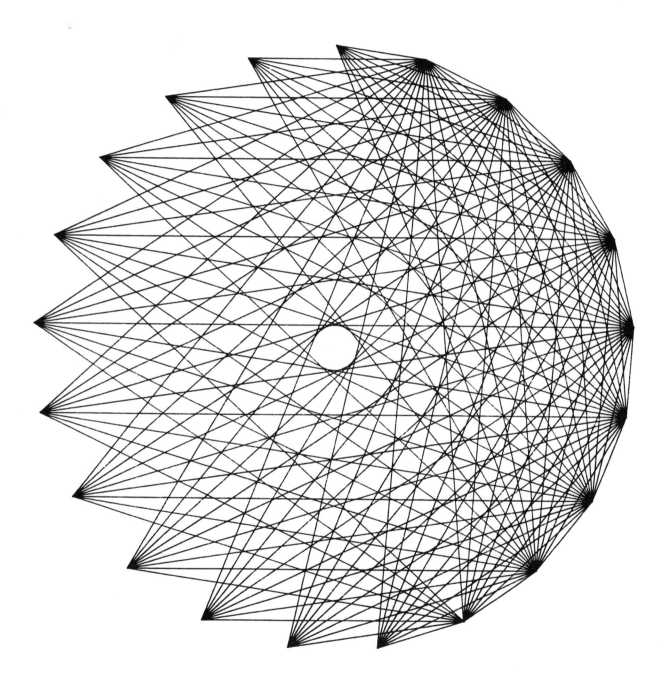

99

Loops (The Way to Keep Things Going)

Because computers need detailed and complete instructions, programs could become very long and full of repetitious commands. Fortunately programmers have a trick that allows the computer to loop back to earlier steps in a program when those orders need to be repeated to get a job done. For example, this is the flowchart for a program called Count 5 that makes the computer display the numbers from one to five.

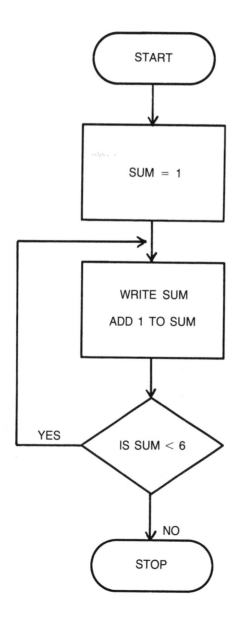

Here is the loop. Follow the directions in the flowchart, counting up the numbers one at a time as you repeat the cycle. How many times do you have to follow the loop before you reach five? Without the loop, you would need to repeat those directions until the sum was equal to five.

To change the flowchart loop into programmed instructions, you need a set of three commands: IF . . . THEN . . . GOTO. The IF command sets up a decision-making situation between two numbers or two variables using one of the decision-making symbols (<, >, =, or <>). When the decision is *true,* the computer follows the instructions after THEN. When the decision is *false,* the computer drops down to the next line number and follows the instructions in that statement. The GOTO command sets up the actual program branch, which is called a loop when GOTO sends the computer back to an earlier line number.

Here is the program written from the flowchart for Count 5. Notice how the commands are used to set up the loop.

```
        NEW
10   S = 1
20   PRINT S
30   S = S + 1
40   IF S < 6 THEN GOTO 20
50   END
```

Try this program on your model computer. When you type RUN and press the RETURN key, write:

1
2
3
4
5

That's the way the computer would display the numbers as it executed the program on your tape.

Now try planning a flowchart and writing a program to make your computer count by twos to one hundred.

Here's another look at Lucky 7:

```
        NEW
10  N = 7
20  FOR I = 1 TO 100
30  PRINT N
40  NEXT I
50  END
```

The trick that makes this program print one hundred sevens is a slightly different kind of loop using a set of two commands: <u>FOR</u> . . . <u>NEXT</u>. There's no decision to be made in this program, and so there isn't a natural branching point. Instead the FOR statement gives the computer a point—in this program I—at which to begin each loop. The 1 TO 100 makes the computer tally up the loops, and each cycle is marked by having 7 displayed as the computer drops down to PRINT N. NEXT I sends the computer back until it has finished the job.

The FOR . . . NEXT loop can be used with string variables too. As the computer loops back to count from one to ten, it also follows the order to PRINT "SCOTT". It will display SCOTT ten times.

Besides the lack of a decision-making step, FOR . . . NEXT loops are also different from IF . . . THEN . . . GOTO loops because they need a code name. In Lucky 7, the code name is I; in this program, it's Z. The NEXT command uses this name to tell the computer where to go back to each time.

```
        NEW
10  A$ = "SCOTT"
20  FOR Z = 1 to 10
30  PRINT A$
40  NEXT Z
50  END
```

Output

RESET: A key on many computer keyboards that, when pressed, stops the program being processed and erases it. Use it with care. RESET also erases everything else in internal memory.

Getting Out and Back In Again

This trick lets you escape a program while it's running. Press the CTRL and C keys on the keyboard at the same time. That's it, you're out.

To get into a new program, type RUN and the program's name. Of course, if you change your mind and decide you want to go on with the program you stopped, just type RUN (or CONT). The program is still in fast memory. When you press the RETURN key, you'll be back in action.

A FOR . . . NEXT counting loop can be varied somewhat by slip-ping in a STEP command. This command is attached to the FOR statement and tells the computer at what intervals the numbers should step up each time.

```
NEW
10  FOR T = 2 TO 100 STEP 2
20  PRINT T
30  NEXT T
40  END
```

With the STEP command, the computer will count by twos from two to one hundred. If the STEP command were to be changed to STEP 3, the computer would count by threes from two to ninety-eight.

The FOR ... NEXT loop also can be used to produce a special effect for your program—a delay loop. Since a computer works in microseconds, it may perform the jobs you programmed so quickly that you don't have a chance to enjoy what's happening. Adding a delay loop will slow down the action slightly.

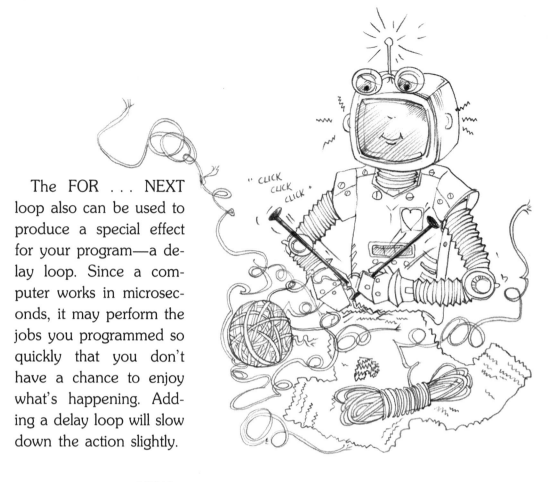

```
          NEW
    10    PRINT "ENTER YOUR FIRST NAME"
    20    INPUT F$
    30    FOR I = 1 TO 10
    40    PRINT F$
    50    FOR T = 1 TO 1000
    60    NEXT T
    70    NEXT I
    80    END
```

Line 50 is a loop nested within the main loop. It takes the computer about one second to run through the numbers one to one thousand. But the numbers are not displayed. The computer wasn't ordered to PRINT these numbers.

Each time this delay loop is completed, the computer drops down to line 70, where NEXT I sends it back up to line 30. Your first name is displayed ten times, with a one-second delay between each appearance. Now try changing the program to give a two-second delay between each word. How about making the computer display your name one hundred times? A delay loop is a neat trick when you want to make every second count.

Tunnel Five

You are walking down the tunnel. Suddenly the flashlight slips from your hand. It clatters on the hard stone floor and rolls away from you. The light goes out.

You get down on your hands and knees. Slowly you inch forward, searching with your hands for the flashlight. Finally you find it. You turn the flashlight on.

"Oh!" you gasp. You are on the edge of a pit. You look down.

The pit is very deep. And it's too wide to jump across. You go back to the cavelike room. You'll have to try another passage.

(Go back to page 12 and try again.)

PEEP!

Peep!

Even short programs can have sound effects if the hardware is designed for it. If your computer's is, type: PRINT CHR$ (7). When you press the RETURN key, the computer will "peep." Like the bell on a typewriter, this sound is a built-in signal. The computer uses the sound to signal an error. But you can also make the computer add this peep with the BASIC command CHR$ (7).

This program will make the computer display HI BOSS and then "peep." Try writing a program that will print the name of your favorite food ten times and "peep" each time the food's name appears on the screen.

```
NEW
10  PRINT "HI BOSS"
20  PRINT CHR$ (7)
30  END
```

My Computer Loves Me

On many computers, holding down the key you want to repeat is the same as pressing it again and again. This program takes advantage of that feature. The number in parentheses at the end of each row tells you how many spaces to leave between the X's. Don't type that number in with your program.

```
NEW
 5 PRINT"          HEART"
10 PRINT"XXXXXXXXXXXXXXXXXXXXXX" (0)
15 PRINT"XXXX      XX      XXXX" (5/5)
20 PRINT"XXXX              XXXX" (14)
25 PRINT"XXX               XXX" (16)
30 PRINT"XXX               XXX" (16)
35 PRINT"XXX               XXX" (16)
40 PRINT"XXXX              XXXX" (14)
45 PRINT"XXXXX            XXXXX" (12)
50 PRINT"XXXXXX          XXXXXX" (10)
55 PRINT"XXXXXXX        XXXXXXX" (8)
60 PRINT"XXXXXXXX      XXXXXXXX" (6)
65 PRINT"XXXXXXXXX    XXXXXXXXX" (4)
70 PRINT"XXXXXXXXXX  XXXXXXXXXX" (2)
75 PRINT"XXXXXXXXXXXXXXXXXXXXXX" (0)
```

When you type RUN and press the RETURN key, your computer will wear its heart on its screen for you.

Light Tricks

You know how to add sound effects to your programs. With some additional commands, you can add lighting effects too.

Normally the print is light and the screen is dark. On an Apple machine, the command IN-VERSE makes the screen light and the printing dark. The command FLASH makes the printing blink. NORMAL returns the screen display to its original form. There are similar commands that work on other machines. Check your computer manual.

The program on the right will make your Apple give you a real light show and "peep" when it's done.

```
NEW
10   P$ = "THIS IS FUN"
20   PRINT P$
30   INVERSE
40   PRINT P$
50   FLASH
60   PRINT P$
70   NORMAL
80   PRINT P$
90   PRINT CHR$ (7)
100  END
```

Shortcuts

A colon (:) can be used to list several statements on the same line. The computer will scan the commands one at a time, from left to right, and do the jobs in that order.

```
Instead of:  10  C = 7 * 2         10  C$ = "CATS AND"
             20  D = C + 6   or    20  D$ = C$ + "DOGS"
             30  PRINT D           30  PRINT D$

Type:        10  C = 7 * 2: D = C + 6: PRINT D
             10  C$ = "CATS AND": D$ = C$ + "DOGS": PRINT D$
```

If you PRINT a message and INPUT a variable on separate lines, you can combine them on one line by using a semicolon (;).

```
Instead of:  10  PRINT "GIVE YOUR FAVORITE TV SHOW"
             20  INPUT T$

Type:        10  INPUT "GIVE YOUR FAVORITE TV SHOW"; T$
```

The computer will display: GIVE YOUR FAVORITE TV SHOW ?

Slipping in Secret Messages

REM means "remarks." It's the BASIC command that lets you sneak secret messages into your programs. Anyone running the program won't discover the hidden notes. These messages are only displayed when someone tells the computer to LIST the program.

If a friend will be using your program, you may want to slip in some surprises, such as the ones in the following program, 5 by 5.

```
    NEW
10  S = 5: REM HI PAL
20  PRINT S: REM WHAT DO YOU CALL A VERY
    POPULAR PERFUME?
30  S = S + 5: REM GIVE UP?
40  IF S < 105 THEN GOTO 20 : REM A BEST
    SMELLER
50  END
```

This counting program will display the numbers from five to one hundred in multiples of five when the computer processes it. When the computer is ordered to LIST, it will display all the secret messages.

Programmers use REM to make notes to themselves. These notes are useful when a program has bugs and a programmer must reevaluate the individual steps.

```
10  PRINT "WHAT IS PRICE?"
20  INPUT P: REM P IS THE PRICE
```

It's important to remember that the computer will not process any commands inserted after REM. If line 20 said: REM P IS THE PRICE: INPUT P, the computer would not display a question mark on that line when it runs the program. Then there would be no opportunity to enter the needed data.

Mini-Mystery

Whew, it was hard getting out. That snow chasm was one hundred and twenty feet deep. Luckily, the bottom was soft, but what a climb. For each minute's struggle, it was a three-foot climb up during the first thirty seconds and a two-foot slide back during the last thirty seconds.

At this rate, how long did it take to get out of the hole? (See page 118.)

GOSUB (It's Not a Dirty Word)

One more trick—this one lets you slip in a little side program without fouling up the main programs. <u>GOSUB</u> is the command that lets the computer jump to another spot in the program and then come back. <u>RETURN</u> is the BASIC command that tells the computer to go back.

Tank Attack

```
NEW
 10  PRINT "THE TANK IS AFTER YOU"
 20  PRINT "YOU CAN FIGHT OR RUN"
 30  INPUT "DO YOU WANT TO FIGHT (Y OR N)"; F$
 40  IF F$ = "Y" THEN GOSUB 80
 50  IF F$ = "N" THEN GOSUB 120
 60  PRINT "TANK WINS EVERY TIME"
 70  END
 80  PRINT "TANK FIRES"
 90  PRINT "YOU ARE HIT": PRINT CHR$ (7)
100  PRINT "YOU CAN'T FIGHT A TANK, SILLY!"
110  RETURN
120  PRINT "TANK ROLLS OVER YOU"
130  PRINT "YOU ARE SQUASHED FLAT"
140  RETURN
```

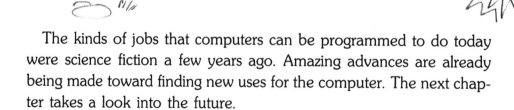

The kinds of jobs that computers can be programmed to do today were science fiction a few years ago. Amazing advances are already being made toward finding new uses for the computer. The next chapter takes a look into the future.

Computers in Your Future

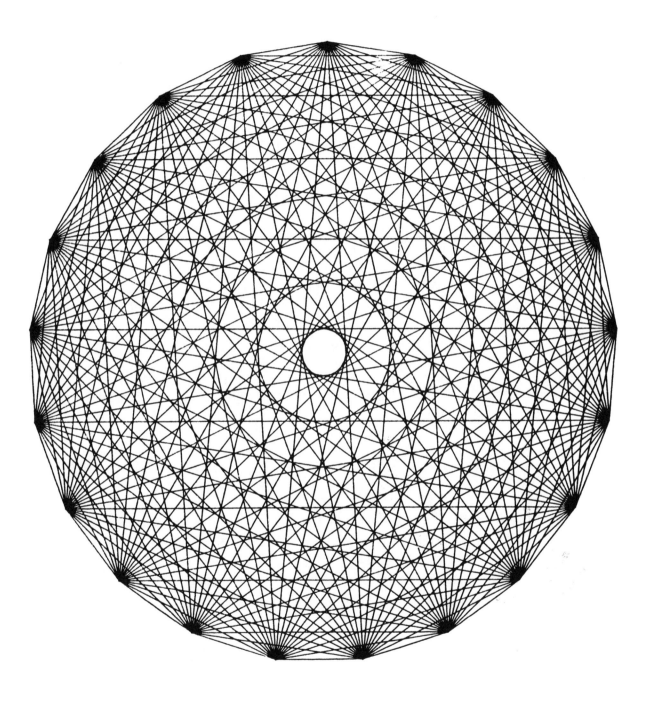

(Courtesy Peachtree Software, Inc., an MSA Company)

Just an Average Morning

The house is dark. It's 5:51 A.M. In exactly nine minutes, the lights will come on and an alarm will go off in your room and in your parents' room.

The home computer changes the thermostat setting from the night temperature to the one chosen for daytime activities. Then it signals the coffee pot to cycle on. Three servings of the omelet mix Mom whipped up last night squirt into microwave dishes stored in the front panel of the refrigerator door.

A radio signal alerts the household robot in the front hall closet. The closet door is pushed open as the Home Helper rolls out. Looking nothing like a movie robot, H-2 has a three-wheeled base and long arms ending in clamp-hands. A laser probe lets H-2 find its way around the house. It receives its programmed commands through the home computer.

H-2 rolls into the kitchen and transfers the three dishes to the microwave oven. The omelets start to bake. When they are finished, the oven will remain on warm until all three dishes have been removed. Suddenly your alarm goes off. *Bzzzzzzzzz!*

"Mmm," you groan after a full minute of the noise. "Okay. I'm awake. Alarm off." The buzzing stops.

You roll over and consider going back to sleep. Then you remember that today your social studies report is due. You finished writing it last night, but you didn't take time to correct it. Pulling on your clothes, you move to your desk.

You boot the computer and bring up your report. A paragraph is needed here. You move the line over. You find a word misspelled. After you correct it, you order the computer to search the text for that word. You want to be sure you didn't misspell it anywhere else. Satisfied, you save the report on your homework disk.

"Morning," Dad calls on his way past your room.

By the time you reach the kitchen, Dad is already eating. The table computer is on. He's reviewing the world news and reading messages that were left for delivery this morning.

"Do you have home study today?" Dad asks. He never remembers which days you stay home for individualized work through the computer.

"Tomorrow, Dad."

Dad looks up. "Want to go bike riding tomorrow afternoon if the weather clears?"

H-2 wheels around you as you take out your omelet. The robot backs up to the kitchen wall and plugs itself into a recharger outlet.

"Sure. I'd like that."

"Like what?" Mom comes into the kitchen carrying a stack of library disks that need to be returned.

"Bike riding tomorrow afternoon," you answer.

"I'll join you." Mom smiles. She plugs the kitchen computer into the modem and begins to type in this week's grocery list.

"Toothpaste," Dad says, stopping to give her a kiss on his way past. "We're almost out."

"Are you going to work already?" Mom asks.

"Have to. I'm going to run through that new program I've been working on. Then I have a meeting at headquarters at ten."

Dad works at home except for business trips and meetings. His office is next to the family room, and his computer system is separate from the household system. He has a direct hookup to the company's mainframe. Most fathers and mothers work out of home offices.

"See you later, Dad," you call. You slip in the new game disk— Strike Force. You operate the joystick one-handed until you finish your breakfast.

Suddenly, Mom reaches over your shoulder and types in a message. "When the computer goes off," she says, "it will be time for you to go to school."

H-2 receives a message from the home computer. Unplugging from the recharger, the robot rolls off to vacuum the bedrooms.

"Just an Average Morning" is science fiction now, but it may not be for long. Computers are already capable of handling most of the jobs mentioned in the story. And as you discovered in "Computers at Work," computers are actually doing many of these jobs.

Home helpers are still in the experimental stage, but robots have proved dependable and useful factory workers. It won't be long before these computer-controlled helpers roll into homes.

What job would you most like to see a robot take over at your house? How would you feel about staying home several days a week for computer-directed lessons?

Mini-Mystery

Mr. Able owns a Christmas tree farm. He decided to experiment with one field to see if he could determine what conditions help produce the biggest trees in the fewest years. To do this he needed to fence his field so that each tree would be separated from the others. He programmed his computer to plan the placement of fences. He wanted to use as few fences as possible to save money.

Here is a picture of Mr. Able's field. The computer was able to use just four straight fences to divide the field, leaving each tree in its own separate section. Copy the picture of the field. Can you figure out where the fences should go? (See page 116.)

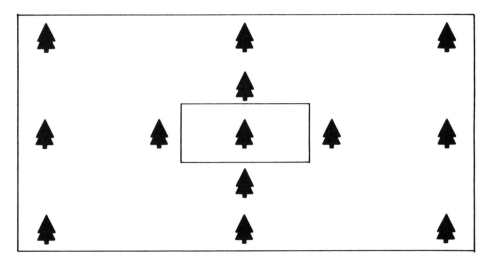

Industrial Robots

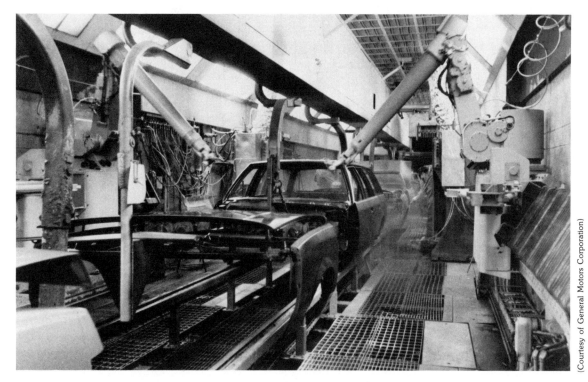

These robots are painting new cars. General Motors has 1,800 robots in use in its plants.

The robots that work in factories don't look like the robots you see in movies. These real robots have long clamp-arms, C-shaped beaks, laser eyes, and infrared probes.

Industrial robots can do the same job over and over, with exactly the same results. They can work overtime without being paid for the extra work, needing a dinner break, or getting tired. To change jobs, the industrial robots don't have to be retrained. A new tool and a new program are enough.

Despite the fact that they are reliable, efficient, and can take over dull and dangerous jobs, these mechanical workers aren't entirely welcomed by human workers. After all, robots on the job mean displaced people. Robotics experts claim that eventually, many new jobs will be created as people are needed to manufacture and maintain the robot labor force. Maybe—it's too soon to judge what effect robots will have on production or employment. But industrial robots will revolutionize how people work and the kinds of jobs people do.

Mini-Mystery Answer

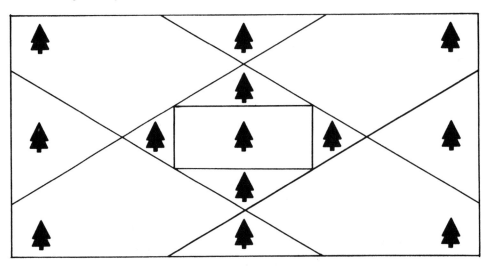

Tunnel Six

You are walking down the tunnel. Suddenly you can't seem to lift your right foot to take another step. Your left foot is stuck too.

You look down. You are standing in quicksand. You're sinking.

You panic. Gasping with fright, you try to struggle to solid ground. All that happens is that you sink faster. You're soon up to your knees in quicksand and sinking deeper by the second.

Forcing yourself to be calm, you stretch out and begin swimming in the soupy mud. Slowly you move closer to the solid edge. When at last you throw one arm onto hard rock, you begin to pull yourself out.

Whew! That was close. Dripping, dirty, and shaking, you plod back toward the cavelike room.

(Go back to page 12. Better luck next time.)

One Important Step Forward

Harnessed for safety, Nan's leg moves in response to signals from a computer.

(Courtesy of Wright State University)

Nan Davis has been paralyzed from the waist down since an auto accident in 1978. After months of muscle- and bone-strengthening exercises, and with the assistance of a computer, Nan was able to rise from a chair on November 19, 1982, and walk about eight or ten feet.

The technology that allowed Nan to walk is based on a computer system and program designed by Dr. Jerrold Petrofsky and his team in the biomedical engineering laboratories at Wright State University in Dayton, Ohio. Electrical signals stimulate ten separate muscle groups, while a feedback system transmits information about muscle and joint positions.

For this walk, Nan was wired to a desk-top microcomputer. Soon this will be replaced by a tiny six-by-ten-inch computer that can be worn over the shoulder. And if experiments go as planned, microprocessors eventually will be implanted under the skin near the paralyzed muscles.

It may be at least ten years before computer-assisted walking is available for large numbers of people. But this is a step forward. The future is full of hope.

In its brief history, the computer has made remarkable technological advances and had a tremendous impact on the way people live and work. From industrial and medical applications to video games and movies full of special effects, computers have not simply changed but transformed the way things are done and what can be done.

If, in the future, computers change only half as much and have only half the effect they've had to date, the results will be fantastic. The computer age has just begun, and the future stretches ahead, full of exciting possibilities.

Did you make it? Did you find the tunnel that held the treasure and let you escape? Did you discover some of the mysteries of computers?

Thanks to the silicon chip, computers have shrunk, become cheaper, and grown steadily more powerful. Best of all, computers have become user-friendly—easy to work with.

Computers are encouraging new creativity. There isn't anything too big or too small to be examined with a computer. You can explore things that seem impossible. You can create three-dimensional models. You can simulate real or fantasy worlds. The computer lets you experiment and discover in ways that are limited only by what you can imagine.

You've entered the computer age at the perfect moment. This important tool has become readily available. It's up to you to find new mysteries to solve and think of new ways to use the computer. The challenges are great.

This is definitely not the end.
This is the beginning.

Glossary

ASCII	American Standard Code for Information Interchange. Used to code all information that is not numbers or arithmetic symbols.
Assembler	Program that translates input that is written in assembly languages.
Assembly language	Language designed to enable programmers to use code words instead of binary code. A special program, the assembler, handles the job of translating the code words into machine language.
BASIC	Beginner's All-purpose Symbolic Instruction Code. Computer language developed by John Kemeny and others at Dartmouth College in the 1960's. It is the most popular language for use on personal computers.
Binary system	Code in the form of ones and zeros that lets a computer store, handle, and process information and commands. The computer uses circuits *on* and *off* (or with high or low levels of electricity) to represent the ones and zeros. The binary number system was developed by Gottfried Leibniz.
Bit	Binary digit. Each bit is one circuit *on* or *off*.
Boot	To start a computer.
Bug	Mistake in a program that keeps it from working.
Byte	Group of eight bits.
Central Processing Unit (CPU)	Integrated circuits that form the processing unit of the computer.
Character	Any letter, number, punctuation mark, or space handled by the computer.
Chip	Tiny, thin slice of silicon with thousands of miniature circuits layered on top of it.
COBOL	Common Business Oriented Language. Designed for writing reports and handling large amounts of data. This computer language is used mainly in business.

Command	Order given to a computer. Commands are most often given through a keyboard, but they may also be given through a light pen (when drawing models or designs), a joystick, or a microphone.
Compiler	Program to translate compiled high-level languages such as FORTRAN. Compiled programs are generally brought in only after the entire program has been typed in the high-level code.
Computer	Machine that can accept, process, and store information or a set of commands. Works best with information that can be described in mathematical terms. A computer cannot love or hate, judge right from wrong, or have an opinion.
CONT	BASIC command for the computer to resume processing an interrupted program.
CTRL C (control key + C)	When these two keys are pressed, it stops the computer's processing action. There may be other keys on your computer that perform this same function. Check your user's manual.
Cursor	Lighted or blinking symbol that is always on a computer screen to mark the next spot where a message will be presented or a symbol will appear if any key is pressed on the keyboard.
Data	Information.
Decimal system	Number system developed by the Hindus that deals with numbers in multiples of tens. It also has zero—a symbol for showing nothing.
Decode	To change from code into plain language.
DIRECTORY	BASIC command to make the computer display a list of programs stored in external memory. Some systems use CATALOG or FILES for this command.
Disk	Looks similar to a 45-rpm record. Used to store information and programs that form the computer's external memory. Material on a disk is not erased when the computer is turned off.
Encode	To change from plain language into code.
END	BASIC command that tells the computer that the instructions are complete.
External memory	Data or instructions stored on a disk, cassette tape, or reel of tape. External memory is not as quickly available to the computer as

ROM or RAM. It is not erased when the computer is turned off.

FLASH
BASIC command that makes the printing on an Apple's video screen blink.

Floppy disk
See Disk.

Flowchart
Graphic outline of the steps needed to do a specific job on the computer.

FOR . . . NEXT
Pair of BASIC commands that set up a way to repeat an earlier part of a program. FOR tells the computer where to start and how many loops to make. NEXT sends the computer back until the job is done.

FORTRAN
Formula Translation. Computer language used mainly in math and science research.

GOSUB
BASIC command that lets the computer jump to another spot in the program, follow a subprogram, and then come back.

GOTO
BASIC command that sets up a branch in a program. When that branch leads back to an earlier step, it forms a loop.

Hardware
Computer equipment on which programs are used.

High-level language
Computer language, such as BASIC, FORTRAN, or COBOL, that uses code words and symbols. "High level" describes their distance from low-level machine language.

HOME
BASIC command that moves the cursor to the upper left corner of the screen and clears the screen on the Apple.

IF . . . THEN
Pair of BASIC commands that set up a way to move to another part of the program. IF sets up a decision-making situation between two numbers or two variables. When the decision is *true*, the computer follows the instructions after THEN. When the decision is *false*, the computer drops down to the next line number and follows the instructions in that statement.

Internal memory
See RAM.

Interpreter
Program to translate interpretive high-level languages such as BASIC. Interpretive languages translate commands one at a time as they are entered or as they are read from memory.

Input
Term used to describe any information or orders given to a computer.

INPUT	BASIC command to make a computer display a question mark and accept data to be stored and used in processing a program.
INVERSE	BASIC command, which works on the Apple computer, to make the screen light and the print dark.
Joystick	Box with a knob that lets you control the movement of a lighted symbol on the screen.
K	1,024, whether bits or bytes. A computer's "intelligence" is determined by the amount of its K—the amount of storage space measured in bytes.
Keyboard	Looks like the keyboard of a typewriter. The most common way to give input to a computer.
Line number	Number that signals the beginning of a statement in a program. Line numbers tell the computer in what order to do jobs. They usually increase by tens so that other lines can be added between them easily.
LIST	BASIC command to make the computer display a program or a line.
LOAD	BASIC command that tells the computer to move a program from external memory to internal memory.
Logo	Computer language named for the Greek word meaning "reason" and "logic." It is used in education and is mainly oriented toward the use of graphics.
Loop	Program structure that makes the computer go back through an earlier part of the program.
Machine language	Binary code, the only way a computer can handle and process instructions and data. (*See* Binary system.)
Memory	The part of a computer where data and instructions are stored so they can be used again. Storage may be in the form of ROM, internal memory (RAM), or external memory.
Microprocessor	Computer on a silicon wafer.
Microsecond	One millionth of a second, the time the average computer takes to work.
Nanosecond	One billionth of a second, the time the fastest computers today take to handle, sort, and process data. At this rate, computers can solve a billion problems per second.

NEW	BASIC command that orders the computer to clear out the information in fast memory and to store the new information that follows.
NORMAL	BASIC command, which works on the Apple computer, to return the screen and display print to their usual form after they have been changed by an INVERSE or FLASH command.
Operating System (OS)	Master control program that directs bringing in other programs, moving data, and processing data.
Output	Response from the computer in usable form.
Pascal	Computer language named after Blaise Pascal. It is designed to solve many of the problems that exist in languages developed earlier and to make programming more efficient.
Peep	Sound used by the computer to signal an error. PRINT CHR$ (7) is the BASIC command that will make the computer "peep" whenever you want it to, if the computer hardware is designed for it.
Peripheral	Any piece of hardware attached to the main body of the computer.
Pixel	Smallest picture element.
PRINT	BASIC command to make the computer display what follows.
Printout	Output from the computer that is printed on paper.
Processing	Rearranging and testing data and performing arithmetic operations.
Program	Set of orders that tells a computer what to do.
Programmer	Someone who gives orders to a computer in computer language.
RAM	Random-access memory, or internal memory. When the computer is turned on, information and instructions can be stored in the CPU's circuits. Internal memory is erased when the computer is turned off.
Read-only memory	See ROM.
REM	BASIC command that lets remarks (notes) be stored with a program.
RESET key	Key on many computer keyboards that, when pressed, stops the

program being processed and erases it. RESET also erases everything else stored in fast memory.

RETURN	BASIC command that, when used with GOSUB, tells the computer to go back to the main part of the program.
RETURN key	Key on the computer keyboard that, when pressed, signals the end of the current statement. A response will then be shown if one has been ordered.
ROM	Read-only memory, or information and instructions permanently stored in the CPU's chips. It is instantly available for processing when the computer is turned on. It is not erased when the computer is turned off.
RUN	BASIC command that tells the computer to look through its memory for a program. Then the computer follows the command on each line, one at a time.
SAVE	BASIC command that tells a computer to move a program from internal memory to external memory.
Software	Computer programs.
STEP	BASIC command that is attached to the FOR statement in a FOR . . NEXT counting loop. It tells the computer at what interval the numbers should step up or down each time.
String variable	Variable that stores words (*see* Variable). A string variable's code name always ends in a dollar sign ($).
SYNTAX ERROR	Computer response to a mistake in the way a command is given or spelled in BASIC.
TAB key	Key on many computer keyboards that works like the tab on a typewriter. TAB lets the computer leap to the right to a new column. It can't be used to go left.
Variable	Stored information identified with a code name. The computer handles finding a location in its circuits to store the information and searches for it each time that code name is used to request the information.
Video screen	Looks like a television screen. It's the most common way for a computer to give output.

Index